camp in Landmannalaugur - Liparit mountains + lava

About this book

Over thirty years ago Gerrit van Gelderen arrived in Ireland from his native Holland and discovered a countryside that had escaped the ravages of the second World War and industrialisation. He brought with him his skills as an artist, his quirky good humour and an energetic enthusiasm for wildlife.

It is our good fortune that he stayed, for he has provided an enormous service in raising consciousness about all aspects of wildlife and especially about the vital aspect of conservation. And he has always done so by entertaining, by expressing and evoking a sense of wonder and enjoyment.

His choice of incidents and expeditions is not a choice of the biggest and the best, nor is he obsessed with rareties. It is characteristic perhaps that he describes a trip to Greenland which was, from the strict "achievement" point of view, a failure. However, one soon discovers in reading his account that it is the wildlife and the people encountered along the way that make his work so richly fascinating both to himself and to his audiences and readers.

This is nothing if not an individualistic book, and the individual we encounter is characterised by a refreshing openness to experience, a relaxed attitude to life and its occasional pitfalls, and a penchant for enjoying and celebrating whatever human, animal, bird or insect life he meets along the way.

The publishers

gerrif van gelderen

to the Waters
and the Wild

BRANDON

third year gannet, turning to dive

First published 1985
Brandon Book Publishers Ltd,
Dingle, Co. Kerry;
and 51 Washington Street,
Dover, New Hampshire 03820, U.S.A.

Text and illustrations © Gerrit van Gelderen 1985

British Library Cataloguing in Publication Data
Gelderen, Gerrit van
    To the waters and the wild: adventures of a travelling wildlife film maker.
    1. Wildlife cinematography
I. Title
    778.5'38591'0924   TR893.5
ISBN 0-86322-077-0

The publishers wish to acknowledge the assistance of Radio Telefis Éireann in
the production of this book.

Typesetting: Fingerprint
Design and make-up: Gerrit van Gelderen
Author photograph: Merlin van Gelderen
Printed in Ireland by Mount Salus Press, Dublin.

contents

Early years

KEET MIELE FOLTJE

ON 1 August 1955, a hot and close day, I first set foot on Irish soil. Unlike Pope Paul I did not kiss the apron of Dublin Airport. I still feel sorry that I did not think of it, for on my very first Irish day, after my very first flight in a real aeroplane, I fell in love with the country.

My relationship with Ireland has had its ups and downs but on the whole whenever I am asked, and this happens with astounding regularity, "Do you ever go home?" my answer is that my home is in south County Dublin and that I usually manage to get there.

I came to Ireland out of curiosity, having answered an advertisement in a Dutch paper for the position of commercial artist in a Dublin advertising agency, Sun Advertising, which is now extinct. Commercial artists are extinct as well: they are now called "graphic designers"; their work, of course, is still the same and often more commercial than art.

That first day I will long remember. All my future colleagues were out at the Royal Dublin Society (RDS) exhibition halls working on a stand advertising a brand of petrol. As my virtuosity with brush, hammer and nails was second to none I started straight away. Finding digs wasn't too difficult and I happily settled into the house of the mother of a colleague. My boss, the late Tim O'Neill, was the nicest man I ever worked for and Dublin life fitted me like a glove.

The time, the middle fifties, was a period of economic expansion. In Ireland there had been hardly any practical schooling available in the fields of advertising and design. Art-teaching was based on the Book of Kells and was ill-equipped to sell airline tickets, butter or even tourism. Foreign artists and designers were imported by the score and I was one of a number of Dutchmen who settled, mainly in Dublin. Most of them are still there, totally integrated into the Irish scene.

I had been born in prosperous, industrialised Holland some fourteen years before the war started. For me there is only one war but I discovered later in Ireland that there have been more and that mine had only been an "emergency" when tea was rather scarce.

The city that rocked my cradle was Rotterdam which, after it had been bombed flat, was to grow to become the largest harbour in the world. Situated at the mouth of the river Rhine and its tributaries which come from the industrial heartland of Europe, Rotterdam handles more tonnage than any other harbour. Goods from France, Germany and Switzerland and far beyond are carried in barges on the European system of rivers and canals and loaded onto sea-going vessels to be sent all over the globe. Between the sea and the city 20 miles inland a vast complex housing the world's largest petro-chemical industry grew up.

1948: Avocet nesting on what is now the biggest harbour in the world

bird watching along the 'Nieuwe Waterweg'

Early bird-watching and botanising was done against an industrial background. In Holland salmon had ceased to come up-river to spawn; frogs were about to disappear in horticultural districts; townships years later had to be evacuated as they had been built on dumps containing deadly chemicals; once common seals were slowly dying out because of pollution of their habitat, and even the provision of clean, chemical-free drinking water for the large cities in the west had become an urgent problem.

I grew up then amidst hustle and bustle but was lucky enough to live out my formative years in a city park. We lived in a small enclave of trees and wildlife, birds and flowers, and the contrast between the park and the busy harbour which surrounded it had a lot to do with my early interest in natural history.

My father's job was in the park. We kept a large number of ornamental fowl, pheasants and peacocks, and in winter cared for most of the city's swans and ducks which were collected in the autumn to populate the ponds in the park. Apart from the Corporation's birds there were always large numbers of wild ones about too:

tufties and scaup, mallard, smews and a whole host of others. There were the normal park-birds as well, from woodpigeons to tits and even nightingales as summer visitors. We had flycatchers, a huge colony of house-sparrows and martins on the house. There were greenfinches and spotted woodpeckers, goldcrests and chaffinches, all breeding within sight of our windows. We had kingfishers, coots and waterhens and often in autumn rarer birds such as waxwings and nutcrackers. It was no wonder that I became an ardent bird-watcher especially after, at the age of eleven, I had joined a Dutch youth organisation for the study of nature.

Rotterdam was, and surprisingly still is not a bad place to see birds. In spring, an hour's ride on bicycle away one could watch ruffs fighting their mock battles along a canal through the polder. There was a marvellous nature reserve called "De Beer" (the boar) opposite the Hook of Holland where the river met the sea. There were unspoiled dunes and a wide green strand and a vast and still rather clean beach. Here was one of the largest sandwich tern colonies in the Netherlands with 17,000 pairs. In autumn it was a paradise for waders; one could watch dotterels at close quarters and sometimes a white-tailed eagle, soaring overhead like a flying carpet, all the way from Scandinavia. In spring there were the breeding birds, small stuff such as nightingales and linnets, all kinds of warblers, colonies of avocets, black-tailed godwits and the other meadowbirds in the polder, common and arctic terns and once even a gull-billed tern, a rare bird which caused great excitement when we found its nest amongst the thousands of sandwich terns. As De Beer was no more than a couple of hours' cycling from home we spent many a weekend there and our organisation made an inventory of the reserve and spent a couple of springs counting breeding birds and doing research in plant ecology.

After the summer of 1940 when the Germans had invaded Holland, De Beer eventually became out of bounds. The Germans changed the place into a large complex of concrete bunkers. After the war the whole area was turned over to building Europoort, the vast harbour complex it is now. Surprisingly enough, though the variety of birds has suffered irreparably, there are still avocets breeding in plenty. The sandwich terns have gone, victims of pollution. I learned to swim in the waters of the river Maas. Nobody swims in the river any more: the Rhine and its branches have become the chemical sewers of Europe, and you'd come out sick and in spots.

Another place where we spent weekends and holidays was the Biesbos "forest of rushes", at the time the last freshwater tidal delta in Europe, a system of islands and rivers with vast reedbeds along the banks and flooded sally-forests, a paradise for birds and anglers, a true jungle in which you could easily get lost.

The Biesbos had been formed in the 14th century when a disastrously high spring tide combined with north-westerly gales breached the dykes and caused the sea to flood great areas of previously reclaimed land and ate a large hole in the Netherlands of the time. Many people and livestock drowned and there are still names in the south of Holland which recall the Saint Elisabeth's flood: names like "Kinderdijk" where according to legend a cradle with a healthy baby inside washed up, saved by the cat who had kept the craft balanced.

Until quite recently no cost-effective way had been found to reclaim the land lost so many centuries ago. Also, as the Biesbos formed an important fresh-water reserve — a scarce commodity in Holland — and was important as a game and hunting domain with rich fishing waters, and a source of reeds and sally, materials for roofing, building and construction of sea-dykes, it had been considered more profitable to keep the Biesbos as it was, a unique nature monument surrounded by the most industrious, intensively farmed and densely populated country in Europe.

Differences between low and high tide could be as much as 6 metres, creating vast banks of alluvial silt brought down with the rivers. Nearer the sea there were more brackish areas with a rich and varied flora and fauna. It was here that we crept in a rickety canoe in winter to spy on the thousands of greylag geese that used the banks to roost after a days foraging in the polder; we discovered a new colony of night herons where there had been no breeding since the last century; we watched the

The experience of my formative years when I saw so many of the things I valued most in life disappear must be one of the reasons I feel so strongly in matters of conservation. It would be a good thing if hardened planners who now are despoiling land- and town-scapes in the name of progress or quick money could have tasted the waters of the Rhine fifty years ago, or seen Europoort as it was before the war and compared with what is there now.

In Holland now, with its dense population in search of a bit of nature, with more and more cars, more and more pleasure craft and less and less space, new lakes are being made for recreational purposes only and agriculturally unproductive land is made into artificial nature reserves where access is totally forbidden or severely restricted.

After the war, in 1945, the Netherlands were left in a shambles, to put it mildly. After five years of occupation, bombing, murder and famine everybody wanted to get away. So, with no more foreign experience than a year in a German slave labour camp and a bicycle trip to Antwerp, all of 65 miles away from Rotterdam, I joined the throng of hitch-hikers and "did" Europe or what was left of it. Hitch-hiking in those days was the accepted form of travel, a new phenomenon. Before the war there had been a hardy band of international travellers who "biapped". That word is long forgotten. It stood for the initials of Bond (league) of International Auto Parasites. These veterans were soon pushed off the roads by all the Toms, Dicks and Henriettas who collected stamps in their brand-new passports without seeing too much of the countries through which they were dragged by sympathetic truck-drivers, American Army personnel and locals in ancient pick-ups.

My first trip was to Scandinavia where some friends and I had been invited by

spoonbills congregating before they set off for warmer climes at the end of summer. Here were still otters, now all but extinct in the Netherlands where their territories have been cut up by roads and railways, cities and industry, isolating the few small populations left and decimating them by pollution and disturbance.

This landscape of the Biesbos is no more. The sea has been tamed and a great barrage stretching along the islands of the southern Netherlands keeps the salt out and the fresh water in. The tides don't run any more and the Biesbos has been tamed. The labyrinth of waterways and lakes separating the islands is there but it has been de-jungled, homogenised like EEC milk. To me the mystery and magic have gone though there are still Kingfishers flashing like bright jewels along the now currentless channels, and the tinkle of the reedlings or bearded tits still sound from the reedbeds. It's all organised, like the rest of neat, prosperous and overcrowded Holland, organised into a yawn. The solitude and freedom of the Biesbos are gone and it is no wonder that I felt happy to be settling in Ireland where there still was and still is wild country, where one can be alone and have a beach to one's self or even an island.

members of a youth organisation to a wildlife camp on the island of Møya in the Stockholm Archipelago. Train fares were beyond our means and in any case one was not allowed to take more than about £2.50 out of the country in foreign money. As an initiation we were transported from Holland to the Danish border in a refrigerated truck, together with some thirty more adventurers. The truck was sealed because of customs but the Thermoking had thoughtfully been switched off. After a cold but sociable sightseeingless party over the late Herr Hitler's autobahn we were all dumped at the Danish border. The real adventure had begun.

At last the war was over and we made it that day to Aabenraa in southern Denmark, in the back of a small truck with dead pigs that added a smelly dimension to foreign travel, and camped that night in a city park in our third-hand ex-army tentlet. For the first time in my life I felt thoroughly "foreign". Few people understood our school English, and Danish proved to be unintelligible though there is a similarity between it and Dutch and we could read it quite well. The Danes, however, are thrifty people: their alphabet has the same number of letters as ours, but they only pronounce three and even those they slur.

Those first few days on foreign soil were very important to me. Rarely ever again, even in much more alien places than neat Aabenraa, have I had this exhilarating feeling of being at the beginning of something totally new, of being at the threshold of discovery and truth.

That feeling faded sooner than later. Learning to understand the Danes and later the Swedes was, after all, not that difficult and most of their English was better than ours. I realised soon enough that it is not language that divides people or makes them different — an observation confirmed later with Eskimos, New York cops, Indian farmers, members of the Popular Front for the Liberation of Palestine, Tuareg tribesmen, Afghan soldiers, Sri Lankan teapickers and officials behind the Iron Curtain. However, I was only twenty and had come through a war which had somewhat warped my judgement, to the extent that there was one proviso left: all people are the same but Germans are an exception. Anyone who spent the war years on the Continent will understand. To others I cannot explain. Anyhow, it is all of forty years ago and now even Germans are included in the fellowship of man.

The Danes being a hospitable crowd, but apparently rarely venturing further from home than twenty miles or so, we swept through Denmark in a series of short jumps, stopping to look for birds and other wildlife, to eat more delicious ice-cream or just to admire the landscape. In the latter respect Denmark was somewhat disappointing. It is even flatter than Holland and just as green and the birds are about the same.

Luckily I was not then and never became a "twitcher", a term I have to explain for readers without ornithological inclinations. Twitchers are bird-watchers who collect birds like others do stamps. Having *seen* a bird, the rarer the better, never mind how briefly or well, is the all-important thing. It can then be entered as a tick on a list. There are county lists, country lists and life lists. The more ticks on your list, the more important a bird-watcher you are supposed to be.

✓ Canada goose
Capercaillie
✓ Carrion crow
Cayuga duck
✓ Chaffinch
✓ Chat
✓ Chiffchaff
✓ Chough
Cirl bunting
✓ Coal tit
Collared dove
✓ Common gull
Common sandpiper
✓ Common tern
Coot
✓ Cormorant
Corn bunting
Corncrake

Well, we didn't keep lists but if we had we would have done well after reaching Sweden. To find ospreys breeding and a white-tailed eagle within sight of Stockholm was a thrill as were our encounters in the lovely landscape of Sweden with all the other forms of wildlife that were new to us: elks and red deer and forest thicker and higher and vaster than we'd ever seen before. We had our camp on lovely Möya which, I believe, has now become just as spoiled and busy a tourist resort as most other fine places in Europe.

Stockholm was a revelation to us. Sweden had been neutral during the war, a fact that a few Swedes we met were rather apologetic about, admitting that they had made money out of Allies and Nazis alike. Coming from war-torn Holland, to be in a country where there were no bombed-out houses, where there was splendid public transport, well-stocked shops, where polished prosperity gleamed at you from all sides, was a thrill. But it was a thrill that soon palled.

Within weeks I had run out of money, so I got a job to tide me over. "Diskare", dish-washing in a restaurant, was not difficult to learn. The work was hard but paid well and soon I had enough to continue travelling. I discovered too that in Sweden hospitals are prepared to pay handsomely for one's blood. The snag was that you could only go to a bloodbank once a month to cash in on half a litre but there is more than one hospital in Stockholm and so I went in every two weeks to sell some of my precious A positive. After millions of dishes and a lot of bloodletting, plus a restitution in cash from the PAYE office, I had enough to continue discovering the delights of Scandinavia which were, and still are, many and varied. I had the choice of going to either Finland or Norway. The choice was easy: for Finland one needed an expensive visa, and the boat fare; Norway was free and could be reached for nothing, as long as you had a thumb.

I liked Norway better than Sweden and felt more at home. The country wasn't as polished as Sweden and the Norwegians had also known war. At the border a large sign read: "You are now entering the Kingdom of Norway where we drive on the right"; just when I had got used to the "first look right, then look left" code. Oslo turned out to be a stern city which I left as soon as possible, continuing to Bergen along one of the most spectacular roads in Europe.

I remember very clearly several incidents in the course of my wet ascent into the highlands of southern Norway. One night, after having been dropped off at some junction in the very centre of absolutely nowhere, I was soaked to the skin. With an icy wind coming down from Norway's largest glacier, Jostedalsbre, I scrambled up some embankment in search of shelter, met the railway and guessed it would lead to a tunnel as most railways do in that part of the world. I found mine after a couple of miles' hopscotching over wet sleepers and settled down for the rest of the night, to be woken

up at intervals by trains thundering past. In the morning it had stopped raining when I emerged into the outside world to the amazement of some railway workers who thought I had walked all the way from Bergen. I must have looked as if I had come from even further. I continued to the railway station, pausing to breakfast on wild strawberries which grew by the pound along the way, and slowly started feeling human again. At the station the stationmaster, who was some seven feet tall by four feet wide pointed out something between the trees higher up the mountain: a real live bear, bigger than I had ever imagined a bear to be. If I had been a mammal-twitcher this bear would have been the prize tick on my life list. Everything seemed to be larger than life in Norway. Years later in Canada I was to see black bears which, compared to brown Scandinavian ones, are nothing but overgrown badgers.

brown bear

13

My experiences at this time were undoubtedly similar to those of anyone who spent summers hitching and occasionally working across Europe after the war. Like others, I worked in restaurants, picked grapes, slept rough, waited for hours or even days for anything on wheels to bring me from A to B or from Y to Z. In the course of my often erratic progress I gained a good working knowledge of the roads of Europe and some of Africa, and in the end my own Z turned out to be Ireland.

exploring Ireland

cock lapwing

FROM the time I arrived, in 1955, I set about discovering Ireland, spending my holidays on the Saltee Islands, exploring the west and south of the country, birdwatching and botanising. I had been lucky enough during my first few weeks on Irish soil to run into John Weaving, an ardent birdwatcher, and it was not long before we went out to Great Saltee, off the Wexford coast, to man the bird observatory, which was mainly run by members of the British Trust for Ornithology.

Saltee is now well-known with serious and occasional birdwatchers alike and is visited by hundreds of people during the summer. In the fifties, however, hardly anybody ever went there, and even arranging the trip over was an adventure. Then as now it was the Bates brothers who brought us over. The island was overrun with rabbits who kept the top as clean as a golf course. That gave lapwings the opportunity to breed and made crossing the island on foot less of a struggle than it is now. Later myxomatosis was accidentally or on purpose introduced and the rabbits declined dramatically, abandoning the "airfield" and old meadows to the weeds and the bracken. Rabbits are great lawnmowers and where they disappear tall vegetation takes over. Saltee is continuously fertilised by the droppings of sea birds and the bracken and thistles are now higher and tougher than anywhere else in Ireland.

We spent many a holiday on Saltee, doing up the old farm belonging to Prince Michael Neil and ringing birds by the hundred. Birdwatching wasn't as popular then as it was to become later and the observatory was irregularly manned, mainly by splendid English chaps. We were often in the pleasant company of Major Ruttledge, the doyen of Irish ornithology.

There was a Heligoland trap, a huge funnel of very rusty chicken mesh, which was stretched out over the few low bushes and trees that constituted the garden behind the abandoned farm. As there was not much in the way of tree cover on the island migratory birds tended to congregate in the garden. The idea was then to "walk them up", slowly chasing them into the narrow end of the trap where they fell into the catching box to be extracted, weighed, measured and ringed and set loose again.

15

a whitethroat in the catching box

Later, when the trap became totally irreparable, we started to use a new-fangled invention, called mistnets. These are nets of very fine black nylon which the birds cannot see, especially when set up against a dark background. Flying into them they catch themselves. A short stay in the net does not harm them at all and this efficient way of catching birds for scientific purposes has practically replaced the Heligoland traps.

the old farm and Heligoland trap

There were few trained ringers in those days in Ireland, but I had been ringing birds in Holland for some years already for the University of Leiden where I had worked, and it was no small thrill to start again in new surroundings on different species. In Holland there are few sea birds breeding.

Razorbill

There are no rocky coasts and islands so there are no fulmars, auks or gannets in summer time. The discovery of seabirds as breeding birds was quite a sensation.

mist netting on Saltee

Stalking a bull seal on Saltee.

The gannet colony on Saltee, totalling many hundreds of pairs and even boasting a fast-growing subsidiary was in its infancy during our first visits and the number of gulls was far smaller than now. The numbers of other sea birds, the guillemots, razorbills and puffins have not changed significantly.

puffin

Saltee has always been our favourite place in Ireland and in 1956 my wife, Lies, and I even spent our honeymoon there. Our next most favourite venue must be the River Shannon. This again was a little less crowded in summer than it is now, and I am still proud that we were among the pioneers of Shannon navigation in the modern sense. John Weaving, as a member of a consortium, had bought an old Dutch life-boat from Willy Bates in Kilmore Quay. That boat, which we named *African Queen* after the famous film, was done up, a kind of a cockpit added and an old car engine installed. To get it to the Shannon took the best part of a week. The Grand Canal was choked with weeds, most of the forty-four locks between Dublin and Shannon Harbour were in bad repair and one had to bring one's own lock key to open the gates along the way. There was one advantage — in those days you could call the canal your own. It was not yet choked with fibre glass floating henhouses full of Liverpudlians or Hamburgers of the angling variety.

Eventually we reached the Shannon where John and partners were to set up a boat hire business. Great fun for everyone involved, resulting in many memorable weekends and holidays, full of corncrakes

17

the glorious summer of '58: down the Grand Canal

and little grebes. The business folded after a couple of years; big capital was invading the river with luxury vessels and the old *African Queen* and her sister vessels, though looking a great deal more friendly and nautical than all the Emerald Stars combined, couldn't compete with more business-like enterprises. John stayed on the Shannon, bought himself an old CIE barge and made it into a floating home-cum--dredger and maintenance vessel. His recognition eventually came in the pages of *National Geographic* where he was nominated "the Grand Old Man of the Shannon" in an article on Ireland full of red-haired children bringing in the turf, round towers and thatched cottages. John also, of course, produced the first Shannon guides and properly charted the river in aid of river tourism.

a great crested grebe, struggling with an eel

My career in Ireland became a chequered one. After some years with Sun Advertising I was lured to the other side of Earlsfort Terrace in Dublin by Paddy O'Keeffe, the editor of the *Irish Farmers Journal*, who offered me a few pounds more and a shorter working week. My task was to illustrate the journal, mainly with cartoons of cows and vast numbers of farrowing crates, milking parlours and graphs showing how much better the Continentals did in dairying. Apart from that I took photographs and started a weekly column on wildlife. Somewhat embarrassed by my Dutch roots I called it "Uncle Seamus's Wildlife Corner". Luckily my English was not printed as it was written but my illustrations needed less editing. Later again I returned to advertising, freelanced as a designer and photographer, worked on promotion in some advertising agencies and eventually talked myself into a job as an art director with a well-known department store in Henry Street. As I didn't seem to be cut out for the retail trade we parted company but by then I was already in the business of popularising wildlife and could look back on the advertising world without regret. Ecologically speaking I had found my niche.

We lived in the bottom flat of an ancient and venerable house on the River Liffey beyond Kingsbridge Station — Sean Heuston Station as it is known within the management of CIE. The house itself, with the romantic name of Edenvale, was falling down around our ears but had the advantage of a cavernous living room with a ceiling reaching well into the stratosphere. There wasn't much else: an endless corridor without the benefit of a bus service to a kitchen of sorts and a bathroom with the largest cast iron bath I have ever had the pleasure of being in. It took a day to fill up and because of that it was impossible to get full with anything approaching warm water.

It made, however, a grand basin in which to rinse photographs. The corridor was flanked with a boarded-up stair-case under which we stored the loads of quaint apples and quinces that came from the delapidated and overgrown orchard. There were also coal cellars which we converted into the dustiest photographic darkroom in Ireland.

no 27 Conyngham Road

The garden and orchard were our joy. There was a jungle of raspberries, there were scrambling roses and even a venerable mulberry tree hanging over the Liffey and dropping its fruit into its murky depths each year. The garden was a bird watchers' paradise and many of my early television programmes were shot there. There were blackbirds and thrushes, bullfinches in the box hedges and flycatchers in the Virginia creeper that kept the house together. Kingfishers sometimes visited the rusty Victorian fountain which we had got working again with the help of a garden hose. We had red squirrels coming to have a look from the Phoenix Park at the other side of the road and once even a red deer which had escaped from the zoo and cleared the wall, and on Wednesdays stray livestock on their way to the cattle market.

To get into this paradise now lost one had to go down through a narrow gate at Conyngham Road and descend fifty-five granite steps to reach river level. It was as secluded and intimate a garden as one could wish for. Beside the house an old conservatory had a real, live vine which never gave anything but a few mouldy grapes, an enormous bush of passionflower, and rose geranium trees. Because there were quite a few holes in the roof — through one of which a sheep once fell — the whole thing resembled Ireland's last remaining rain forest.

A corner of it we had made into an aviary in which we kept some foreign birds and not a few native ones bought at the bird market behind St Patrick's Cathedral — linnets and redpolls and the occasional goldfinch. These birds were usually set free after a while if they didn't escape all by themselves. Security measures were not very strict and even a number of foreign birds — green cardinals and budgies — had the freedom of the garden for long periods. It is, in fact, those birds that were the cause of me ending up with a television programme on Radio Telefis Eireann (RTE).

The old garden was our constant joy. We didn't make much effort to tidy it up though once we acquired a goat, called Emma, to keep the grass down. This method of biological control is not to be recommended: goats prefer ornamental shrubs. Once some travelling people pushed a billygoat through the gate and we were looking forward to having other kids than our own on the premises. Unfortunately, probably because of conditioning during his deprived youth, Billy didn't make any advances to Emma but preferred indecently assaulting terrified visitors. One day we took the goat by the horns and set him loose in Phoenix Park. There he started to celebrate freedom by charging two cyclists. Later that week he made it to the front page of the *Evening Press*: a three-column photograph of him walking into the Metropole cinema, O'Connell Street, no doubt to see an X-rated film.

There was really no need to keep animals. Kingfishers flitted along the Liffey. They bred somewhat higher up, and though we never saw the animals themselves, otter tracks were a regular feature in the mud at low tide. Seals came up now and then, especially when the salmon were running. We could see those passing by as dark shadows on their way to the weir at Islandbridge where they would mount the salmon trap past the pool. The salmon were sometimes followed by seals, which passed unnoticed through the city. We loved the seals, and I will never forget the one that surfaced just in front of the garden with a salmon in its mouth, winking at me.

Mullet came up as far as the house and once during a dark night we spanned a wadernet across the river — totally illegally of course, but I hope that this crime is now forgiven. It was hard and smelly work which resulted in the catching of one single mullet

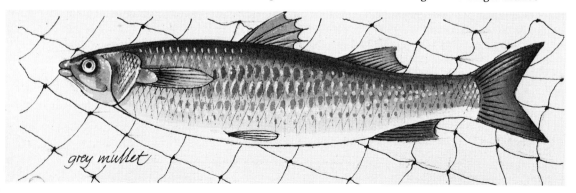

grey mullet

which we transferred to the fountain where it got fat for a while before committing suicide by jumping out. There were others, and probably still are along that stretch of river, who had a more business-like and sustained approach to poaching.

We kept pets of all kinds. Apart from our mullet in the pond and the birds in and out of the aviary we had a succession of rabbits, hamsters, foxes, hedgehogs and a brent goose, for these were the days before the Wildlife Act. We became ardent photographers as well, with the locals as subjects: blackbirds on their nest, robins and tits on the bird-table and butterflies on the weeds. I never managed to get a shot of our kingfishers — their visits to the garden were too sporadic and along the banks of the river it was simply too dark and mucky.

We had a boat, an old currach which we had bought for six pounds from Richard Murphy, the poet. On Sunday mornings we used to row down to O'Connell bridge, attracting no end of attention and rude remarks from passersby, moor at the bridge, give some boy a tanner to look after our craft, and have coffee at the Gresham, with the Liffey smell still clinging to our rubber boots. Maybe we caused some comment but were never thrown out. They were used to eccentrics, and probably still are.

pet fox-cub

One day John Molloy and Barney McKenna called for a loan of our craft in aid of some publicity stunt. They went down the Liffey in it, but near O'Connell bridge, in urgent search of refreshments, forgot to tie it to the wall properly, which resulted in a phone call from the lighthouse: was it our boat that was following the *Leinster*? Fortunately we got our currach back and had more adventures in her, around Saltee and Roaninish and Slieve League in Donegal.

cruising down the Liffey

getting into television

THE programme, *Amuigh Faoin Spéir* came about because of the birds I kept. I had met Éamon de Buitléar when he was just married; Laille and he ran a small pet-shop in Parnell Street and it was there that I bought food for my birds and animals. Éamon was deep into Irish music and I was an artist, photographer and amateur naturalist. I was working at the time as a visualiser at Janus Advertising, in Parnell Square, just around the corner from their shop.

When in the early sixties Radio Telefis Éireann began putting the "téléfis" part into practice Eamon and I discussed how we could make an Irish music programme, enlivened with drawings and a bird here and there. We had only the vaguest notion of how to develop our ideas. All the same we went down to Donnybrook and saw Maeve Conway, the head of children's programmes. However, she was less enthusiastic than we were and she turned us down.

It was not the first time that I had been in contact with the newly established television service. I had, together with practically every designer in Ireland, applied for the advertised job of art director. Mr Roth, a Canadian and controller of programmes of the day, had interviewed all the applicants at intervals of a quarter of an hour, so everybody had met everybody else in the hall of RTE where we had quite a party.

When our idea for an illustrated music programme was not accepted I mooted the idea that we should try again and this time base our proposals on my own hobby, wildlife. Ireland in those days was not exactly wildlife minded and the notion that a public might enjoy watching the natural world was not one that had forcibly struck controllers of programmes. All the same, the idea was accepted and we got our little slot, a weekly thirteen minutes on a Sunday afternoon. We were allocated a producer and the whole crew of Studio One would be at our disposal.

That first *Amuigh Faoin Spéir* was to be about swans. I had caught one previously on the Liffey, which probably even then had been illegal. I constructed a wooden frame of immense dimensions, covered it in netting and hung it out over the river. The local swans were used to being fed and with the help of some bread I succeeded in enticing one underneath my contraption. As it had been quite a struggle to get the bird out of the net and the river-muck it wasn't exactly a clean swan that arrived at Donnybrook on that first Sunday afternoon.

We went through the hands of a series of producers. One of the first was Louis Lenten, who didn't have much sympathy for the subject, or if he ever had it, soon lost it when birds escaped into the large studio, so-called tame squirrels climbed the curtains, and mice ran all over the place. Some of the RTE boys must have dreaded seeing us coming in with yet another sample of Ireland's fauna which was likely to bite, make itself invisible at crucial moments or simply fly or run away.

It became clear that this was not the way to show wildlife, that we had to go out and film the real thing instead of bringing in pets or illegally procured waterfowl. For our first film, then, a cameraman was dispatched to get us some footage on house-sparrows; we were not allowed or probably thought capable of doing the job ourselves. Unfortunately, to film birds, even house-sparrows which are not that difficult to find, is an

acquired skill if your life hasn't been bird-orientated, so the film we got was not exactly up to standard. Still, there must have been sparrows on it, somewhere.

I was the owner of an old Bolex cine-camera which I had bought one day after a well-paid nixer, long ago. Up to then I had been making family epics on an 8mm camera. I had discovered quickly that I couldn't afford to shoot expensive 16mm film in any quantity, so the camera had not been used much, but it was with that Bolex that we went out to get our first very own programme together on Bull Island in Dublin Bay, then as now one of the easiest places in the whole of Ireland to shoot birds. We did not have a tele-lens or even a proper tripod but somehow managed to get enough oyster-catchers and recognisable ducks together to fill more or less our allotted time. The holes I plugged with drawings.

My coal cellar had been promoted to studio and in the doorway I had constructed a glass frame, against which we stuck news-print. Behind it a set of lamps and me, drawing away with a fat felt pen that made nice thick lines. The whole thing we filmed from the front, and so "live" drawing was born. The idea was not exactly new for I had seen on film Picasso doing it in the same way, but at least he didn't fill his sheets with maps of bird-islands or the differences between a razorbill and a guillemot. There were some difficulties to overcome, mainly centring around letters such as S, Z and R which are hard for a beginner in mirror-writing; it is quite impossible to formulate captions with only Os or other letters that look the same from any direction. Ever seen a ЯОᗺⅠᴎ ?

I learned fast and we found that what had begun as a means of filling awkward gaps in continuity was very much liked by our view-ing public. It also eventually gave the pro-gramme its own character. We still shot in black and white which made life somewhat easier than it is now. There is a convenient latitude in exposure which in practice means that you can film in far more difficult and darker circumstances than is possible with colour film. The commentary in both Irish and English also proved successful, though we had endless correspondence with people who either wanted the whole thing in Irish or all in English.

Altogether we had found the right format. We also acquired some more and improved equipment and it was now possible to get better close-ups of birds and animals. It must be said that in the early days of RTE there was not yet the wealth of brilliant wildlife films available to which the public is used today. I wouldn't dare any more to have an oystercatcher walking around the screen for two minutes doing nothing but if there are still people in Ireland who don't know what an oyster-catcher or for that matter a brent goose looks like, it certainly was not our fault. For the rest we made expeditions to Saltee and filmed sea-birds, to the late Tern Island in Wexford Harbour, to the Wexford Slobs for the geese, came home with magpies picking wool off cows; in short, did all the obvious things.

We started to discover that insects and flowers and smaller things also made good television. We travelled all over the country. Éamon in the meantime had also acquired a camera and we ended up filming different things in different locations, and did not work as closely together any more. We had to produce forty-eight programmes a year, which swallowed film at a fantastic rate, and this was one way to get variety. The editing, scripting and dubbing was done together and we didn't change the format or let on who did what, and all pro-grammes carried the same credits.

The controller of programmes of the time, Gunnar Rugheimer, had given us a longer "slot" requiring something for anglers too, which eventually was forgotten. In the meantime we were doing other things for RTE as well. We made shorts on any old subject from Irish insects to "Newsbeat" and I was busy doing my "live" drawing act to go with the News.

RTE also started a new programme for farmers, called *Telefís Feirme*, of which I have the most pleasant memories. It was hosted by Justin Keating, like me an improviser, and produced by Seamus Smith, a man of no mean adaptability. He certainly needed it. I did the animated graphics, and my years with the *Irish Farmers' Journal* came in handy. If, for example, milk yields in European countries were under discussion — a recurring subject — I would be standing behind a screen, invisible to the cameras, pouring milk into a row of empty bottles forming a graph and as if by magic the levels rose from the front. The programme was full of smiling cows, caricature pigs and once we had a funny plywood sheep giving birth to a rubber lamb, deftly assisted by Justin who, after all, started life as a vet. The series, because of its unusual and original format, was a winner and when it received the Jacob's Award I was quite proud to have been a member of the team.

By that time I had moved from the ruins of our part-mansion along the Liffey to a new house in the Dublin mountains. I did my work in a basement studio in Blackrock which was a most convenient venue: when driving to Donnybrook from there one had to pass Booterstown marsh which was always good for a few more snipes, dunlin or even oystercatchers. There were also the grounds of University College Dublin (UCD) along the way where one could demonstrate ringing blackbirds, early spring flowers or toadstools. I had

acquired staff too: Susan, straight out of school, who for five years drove the old landrover, kept the books, brought film to processing, loaded cameras, made coffee and became the most popular production assistant ever, not only in Blackrock but no less so in the hallowed halls of Donnybrook itself.

One day during a bank strike, Oscar Merne, a young employee of the Bank of Ireland blew in. As he was also an ardent and knowledgeable bird watcher, he became part of the team and never went back to the bank. Later David Shaw-Smith joined the ranks.

Amuigh Faoin Spéir had become an institution and we duly got our own Jacob's Award for the best home-produced programme of the year. I say "duly" for if you are on the list of programmes long enough eventually you reach the top when all the others have had their trophy. So Éamon and I, all dickied up, for once stood in the limelight at a memorable party in the Jacob's factory on George's Street which, like so much else in Dublin, is no more. Ireland was our field of exploration, but as we were required to fill such a lot of time with interesting material, most of our programmes were of a rather journalistic nature. Not that there wasn't enough of interest to film in Ireland which, after all, was still one of the least spoiled and least polluted countries in Europe, but to make wildlife films in depth an abundance of time is of the essence.

If one wanted to film the life-cycle of some animal or bird, one would need a year in the field at least. We had to produce a dozen or so shows annually, so we had only a couple of weeks to make each one, and we had to become opportunists. A way out might have been so-called head and shoulder television where some key-man fills time by talking into a camera. But I prefer a film about seals to show seals and their habitat only, and not somebody talking about them against a sealy background. Good subjects for films with commentators talking *off* rather than *on* screen were fishing trips, visits to wildfowl collections — we went several times to Peter Scott's famous place in Slimbridge — nature reserves and bird islands. At such places one did not concentrate on a single species but was able to make a lively programme by showing great action or variety.

The most important element of wildlife film making is that you know your subject, that you do your homework and need not rely on lucky breaks. If you get those, of course, they are a bonus: if a stoat turns up when you are filming rabbits, or a rare wader amidst a vast flock of very common ones, or if you catch an exotic triggerfish in Loughine when you were only expecting mackerel, then you exploit the unusual.

With a career based on what had been my hobby, I found that I could explore the world of wildlife to my heart's content. I loved to walk at night through a deserted landscape. And it remains a great joy to walk alone in a place like Saltee Island when all is dark and silent, apart from the murmurings of the sea, the sleepy noises of the sea birds, and the song of a startled sedge-warbler who needs no more than a rustle in the bracken to react. The idea too that you are all on your own and there is nobody else for miles around is exhilarating in itself. One becomes attentive to the simple sounds of the night, the rustle of a mouse in the undergrowth, the call of far-away waders, or when on the mainland, the sniffling shuffle of a badger in the undergrowth, the whistle of sika deer, the high, thin shrieks of shrews having an argument. There are no visual distractions, though it is amazing the things you can see at night

when your eyes have become tuned in to the dark: the silent hovering of a barn owl hunting for mice or the silhouettes of migrants high above.

One night in Donegal where we were staying in a caravan near Kiltoorish Lake I was tramping the fields in the dark during a slight drizzle. Corncrakes were calling all around me — these were the days before they became so scarce. There were no sounds other than the persistent rasp of the birds, an ideal night to record them. So I did, and then sat down in the wet to play it back and give them a dose of their own medicine. Hardly was the tape recorder switched on when a corncrake came tumbling out of the sky on top of me. Of course I grabbed it and brought it to the caravan to show to Lies and ring it. If that worked at night, it should work in daylight as well, I thought, so next morning the mirror was unscrewed from the caravan, put up against a tall ragwort and the recorder put behind it, while I retired a couple of paces with the camera to see what would happen. The corncrake could now see me and although more hesitant was soon out and, seeing his reflection in the mirror and sensing a competitor in his territory, put up a terrific fight with his image up to the moment that the mirror fell over on top of him. Luckily no harm was done, at least not to the corncrake.

Tape recordings of birds and animals are used more and more to get them close, unfortunately also by poachers for more sinister purposes than to get a photograph or a bit of film. Hunting foxes with sound as a bait has become commonplace. Years ago a lady sent me a tape with the title "El Canto del Perdiz" which she had bought on holiday in Spain. Instead of the flamenco she had expected there was nothing on it but the call of a red-legged partridge, twenty minutes of it; the tape had been meant for local hunters rather than tourists.

If one is sitting, as I love to, at the edge of some marsh or mudflat watching waders and wildfowl and there is this one bird on the other side of the opinion that your side of the marsh is inferior, often all you have to do is to play back the bird's call and it will come within reach of the camera. That works well though bird brains are not all that gullible. If you get your spotted redshank or whatever over a few times it will soon discover that it is being cheated and ignore any further attempts. The volume of the sound need not be high. Birds have far better hearing than humans and pick out the calls of their own species infallibly from amongst the loudest of background noises. You need not have a perfect recording either: birds are less critical than Hi-fi fans. It is through sound, too, that we can discover birds where we thought there would be none. During migration time playing back the charming sound of breeding storm petrels along a beach one can entice flocks of them inshore when they were first travelling along the coast miles out, unsuspected by bird watchers.

spotted redshank in summer plumage

It was inevitable that in making the programmes over the years we gained a better and more intimate knowledge of the country than most. We went to outlying islands such as the Blaskets and the Skelligs, explored the Shannon from source to sea and went to many places in seasons when no sane person would ever think it worth the trouble. Going out to Skellig Michael in the past was quite an adventure and called for some organisation. During recent summers, however, thousands of people have gone there and also to the Great Blasket where there is now a regular boat service and one is no longer dependent on the goodwill of a local friend to bring you and the gear over. There is a constant dilemma, in that the more you make publicity for places you value, the more there is a chance that they are going to be spoiled for ever.

stormy petrel

Merlin

The Gerrit and Éamon team produced a stream of programmes, season after season. We each did our own shooting, editing and script writing; Éamon spoke the commentaries and I looked after the graphics. The credits never divulged who did what, and this sometimes led to me being complimented on the excellence of my Irish and Éamon on his skills as an artist. We were often on the road for weeks on end and schedules sometimes clashed, so each of us started to do his own thing and we gave up producing shows as a twosome. Somehow, however, the public could not forget the combination of the old days and have kept on linking our names, even now, more than ten years after we separated.

I faced the difficulty of trying to continue my programmes in the same old mixture of Irish and English; Gabriel Rosenstock, a budding poet and broadcaster, joined me to translate and act as commentator. This worked for a while but had the disadvantage that I couldn't understand half of what I had written. It was Muiris MacConghail, now Controller of Programmes in RTE, who suggested that I should not only write but also speak the commentary myself, never mind my irreparable Dutch accent. I had never been able to say anything sensible into a microphone before, but after a while I got into the swing of it and nobody seemed to mind my accent — another example of the sometimes amazing tolerance displayed by the Irish. Not being able to speak in a Cork, Kerry or Dublin accent has some drawbacks. Ordering a pint in a pub, I am usually asked, "Aren't you the fellow that does the birds on RTE?" My voice is instantly recognised, but I have ceased being touchy about it. After all, I am too old for elocution lessons.

The Controller of Programmes of the day decided one day that the programme title *"Amuigh Faoin Spéir"* had had its run and this really was the end of the old series.

Every other television station was now producing its own wildlife programmes and to find a catchy new title was rather difficult. All the obvious ones had been appropriated — wild world, world about us, wildlife on one or two, survival, and no mean number of safaris of all sorts. I drew up a whole list of possibilities, each one cornier than the next, and was about to submit them to Donnybrook when an old friend, John Fogarty from Cork who had been on several wild world safaris with me, happened to drop in, studied my efforts and quoted Yeats:

> *Come away, O human child!* ✱
> *To the waters and the wild*
> *With a faery, hand in hand,*
> *For the world's more full of weeping*
> *than you can understand.*

and that was that. I never looked back and hope to be able to continue for many years to come.

After the success of my first trip to Iceland, which resulted in a series of four interesting programmes, and forays into the Sahara in the following years, shooting wildlife abroad as well as in Ireland became a compulsive habit. The budgets on which independent film makers work are not lavish, to put it mildly, and travel had to be done on the cheap. Sometimes one was able to get some sponsorship in the form of free or cut-price tickets from airlines and travel agencies, and this helped. The least cumbersome way of going anywhere was, and still is, to throw everything in the back of a van equipped with bunk, cooker and tent and set off, together with some other sympathetic soul who doesn't mind roughing it either.

✱ *from W. B. Yeats: "The Stolen Child"*

28

So I visited all the countries around the Mediterranean apart from Libya, only going to Lebanon and Syria by plane. It is very convenient to be the guest of some government department, but it can also be quite a strain to be under obligation to hosts. Invariably housed in hotels, you have to go through all kinds of formalities of which breakfast is the most agreeable and least time-consuming.

All sorts of strange things can happen when you travel independently with a film camera. One Sunday in Sidon I was arrested by members of the Palestine Liberation Organisation (PLO) who just couldn't believe that my camera was aimed solely at things natural and ancient and that I had not been sent by the people south of the border. After an hour's interrogation and stern banter they let me go but first

they served me a nice meal with assurances of eternal friendship for all things Irish.

On the same trip, at Baalbek, a man offered to supply me as much hash as my car could carry. I refused his offer but he proved to be a knowledgeable guide and an admirable host. He showed me the family's armoury which to me seemed enough to arm a company of soldiers. When I enquired if all these Kalashnikovs and other obnoxious hardware were meant to be used against the Israelis, I was told that some of the neighbours would be more likely targets. At the time I didn't take that seriously but the following year civil war broke out and it had probably been true.

Sadly, almost everywhere I go trouble breaks out. The Lebanon was a case in point as, much later, was Sri Lanka. After I had driven through Afghanistan the Russians

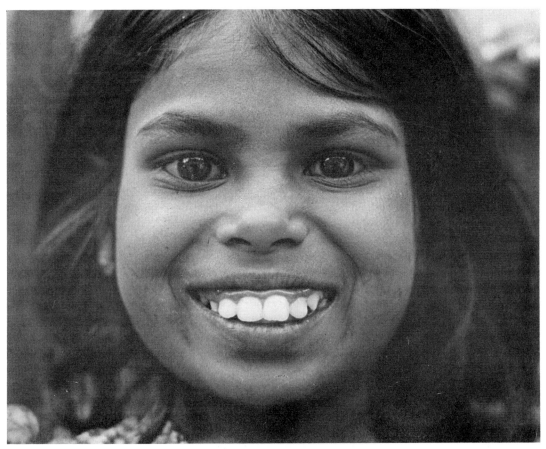

my favourite photograph: a Tamil child on Sri Lanka

29

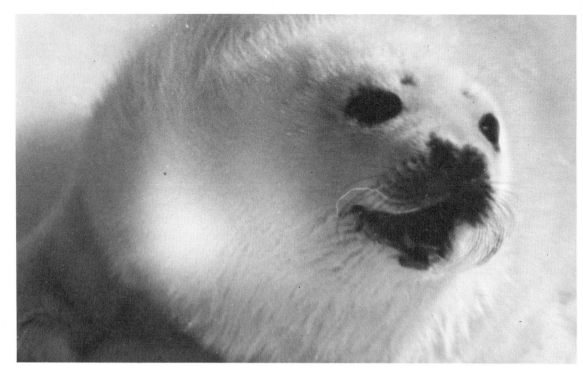

A harp seal pup and the remains of another one, killed and skinned by a Canadian sealer.

Dettifoss, Iceland's and Europe's largest waterfall.

moved in, and in the Punjab there is trouble again too, not to speak of the Western Sahara where an insidious war is being waged between Moroccans and the Polisario.

But then, the Arctic seems to be as pristine a place as it ever was. I don't think that politics will keep me at home, nor will minor inconveniences deter me. Once, with a ticket to Canada in my pocket, I had been so clever as to break an achilles tendon when on Crete I was trying to dance a sirtaki. Not wanting to miss out on the opportunity to see Canadian gannets instead of Irish ones and to see the Pacific for the first time, with my leg in plaster, I went all the same.

I went to Canada again later to film the harp seals which pup on the pack-ice coming down from the Davis Strait into the Gulf of Saint Lawrence. I arrived in Charlottetown on Prince Edward Island during a raging blizzard which lasted for three days and made further travel impossible. Also cooped up in the small hotel were David Attenborough, John Sparks, the producer of BBC's 'Life on Earth', and a camera crew, there to hopefully record a sequence on the birth of a seal. At last, when the weather turned, we all flew out to Magdalen Island in the sun, where the seals on their pack-ice had been blown against the shore, and there I saw a lot of the whole revolting bloody business of the seal "cull". When later our footage was made into a film, I tried to preserve some balance and didn't go into hysterics. In any case, my surreptitiously obtained shots of skinned carcasses and trails of blood spoke their own story and did not need the addition of men yielding their clubs or my verbal indignation.

Over the years seals have become my favourite wild animals and if ever I become a Buddhist or embrace some other belief which promises reincarnation I want to be a seal. I'll take good care to stay away from

An Irish grey seal, playing with her pup on Carrigawilt, Co. Mayo

eastern Canada, or for that matter the Inishkeas in County Mayo. To be shot by an eskimo to feed his family wouldn't be too bad: I will turn into a gannet then — I love fresh mackerel.

Neither David Attenborough, nor I got our seal-birth pictures. Standing on the ice surrounded by a herd of sleek and fat expectant mothers who in no way look different from those that already have given birth, it is only by pure chance that you'd catch the few seconds it takes a baby seal to see the light of day. Maybe I'll succeed one day on Saltee and then RTE may have the scoop.

Land of Ice and fire

FROM the very beginning of the television series I had realised that one day I would have to stretch my wings, not only because I had always been in search of new horizons but also because the wildlife of Ireland and thus its conservation cannot be seen as something isolated. In order to bring home the message that wildlife knows no borders I would have to travel myself. After all, our brent geese come from three thousand miles away; they breed in Arctic Canada. The white-fronted geese which we had filmed so many times on the Wexford slobs breed in Greenland, and the swallows that have their nests in Irish barns spend the winter in South Africa. We get Whooper swans from Iceland and Bewick's swans from Siberia. Huge numbers of waders and waterfowl come from continental Europe. Of course, not only birds migrate: in summer we get many butterflies from southern Europe and even Africa.

My first choice for an extended trip was Iceland, our nearest neighbour in the North Atlantic, from where so many birds travel to our shores at the beginning of winter. Iceland has a remote ring to it but if you look at a map it isn't really that far away.

How Iceland got its cold name is no more than an accident of history. A Swede by the name of Gardar discovered the country quite by mistake. He had been on his way to the Hebrides to claim some property his wife had inherited but he never made it as he ran into a gale that swept him 600 miles to the north-west. There his longboat ran onto a lava beach. Sailing around the new-found land he realised that he had discover-ed an island and a large one at that. He spent the winter at Husavik, the Bay of the House, and next summer sailed home to sing the praise of 'Gardar's island'.

The story caused some excitement in Sweden as well as in Norway and another enterprising Viking, called Floki, set out to see for himself and settle. He equipped his boat, put his two daughters aboard, three ravens, a couple of cows and horses, some dogs and food for the lot and set off. First port of call was the Shetlands where one of the daughters met with an unfortunate accident and drowned in a lake which to this day still bears her name, Girlsta Water.

Floki continued to the Faroes, the Far Islands, married off his remaining daughter, and turned north. After a couple of days one of the ravens was released. It flew straight back to the Faroes. After another couple of days raven number two was let go; it circled the ship a few times and settled on deck again. Floki concluded that they must be halfway. Later the third raven headed north and did not return. Soon Iceland came in sight.

Floki Vilgerdarson settled at Barda-strand and spent all summer fishing and harvesting winter fodder for his livestock. The following winter was a very severe one and the fjord filled up with pack-ice. Life became impossible and Floki went home again as soon as he could, having no good to say about his Ice-land.

A Saltee gannet and Little Skellig with the second largest gannetry in the world.

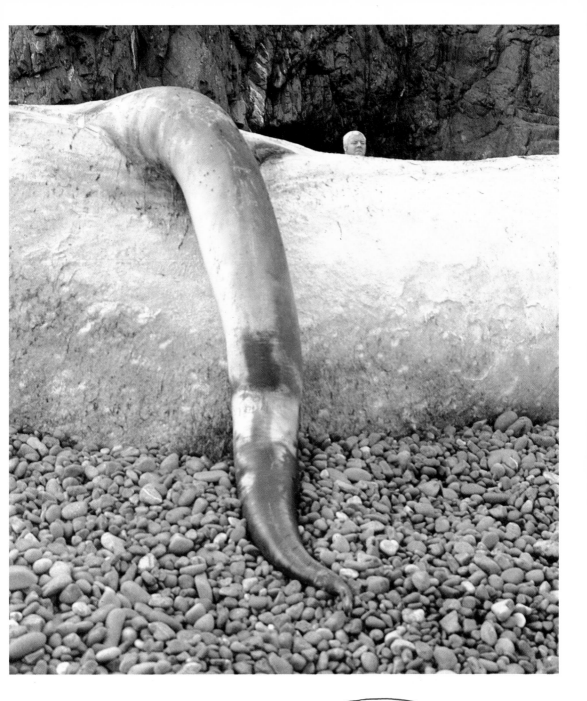

Large whales often pass unnoticed along Irish coasts; sometimes a dead or dying one washes up, like this 60 ft. male rorqual or fin whale which came ashore, much damaged in county Waterford in 1983. It must have weighed over 40 tons. The area around Ireland has been declared a whale sanctuary where killing of any whale (or dolphin) is illegal — a laudable gesture but in practice hard to enforce.

Iceland was at the time going through a spell of very bad winters, much colder than they are now. The weather in the North goes in cycles, a number of good summers alternating with cold ones and very severe winters. A difference of only one or two degrees centigrade in the average temperature during a succession of summers may bring profound changes in animal populations. Starlings and swallows, for example, have only arrived in Iceland since the 1950s. During a stretch of warm summers, too, cod will travel much higher north which for a country as dependent on fish as Iceland is very important.

After the first failure of colonising Gardar's island or Floki's Iceland many more ships departed from Norway and the country became a Viking colony. Around the ninth century Irish monks had settled on the south-west coast but as the birth rate amongst celibate monks is negligible, the Irish had died out. Centuries later Hjorleif, one of the first Viking settlers, ran out of supplies after his first winter and returned to Norway to stock up. From there he first sailed to Ireland to do some shopping in the Viking way and after a round of monasteries came back to Norway again with a fortune in booty and ten Irish slaves. Two ships were fitted out and a brother by the name of Ingolf was persuaded to return as well. Then, loaded with household goods, livestock, slaves and freemen it was off for Iceland again to found a new nation.

Ingolf was a very conscientious pagan who had duly made offerings to Odin before departing from Norway. Hjorleif, however, had seen something of Christianity during his Irish days and refused to join in the sacrifices — to his peril. In those days it was still Thor and Odin who governed Iceland rather than the Lutheran Church. The brothers had a row and parted company. Ingolf set up business at the Bay of Steam, Reykjavik, and became a success whilst Hjorleif, in true Christian spirit, was murdered by his Irish slaves around the year 874. So, from the very beginning Irish blood was present in the Viking colony and Irish genes are still rampant among the 200,000 Icelanders of today.

The Icelandic language is a difficult one: it is not just another Scandinavian tongue but a carefully preserved form of Old Norse, kept pure through the centuries. But because very few people speak it outside Iceland, for practical purposes English is taught in primary schools, which means that there are no problems of communication for the visitor.

In planning my trip to Iceland I was aware that it possessed the advantage of nearly touching the Arctic Circle, which meant that in summer we would have light practically night and day and so could cram an enormous amount of filming into a working day. I wanted to take my own transport to the island. The old VW van which had served me well was creaking at the

Eldfell on the Vestmannaeyar, a brand-new volcano.

seams and would probably fall apart halfway up a volcano of which they have great numbers in the land of ice and fire. None of the roads on Iceland are metalled and what we needed was a four-wheel-drive vehicle, so I bought a brand-new Landrover.

Having little or no experience in such a car, and in the mistaken belief that there are no limits to what they can do, on our first trial run onto the muds of Bull Island we sank into the mire. She had to be left overnight at the mercy of the tide for the driver of the tractor at St Anne's Golf Club, much used to dealing with hapless Sunday drivers, flatly refused to be as stupid as we had been. The next day we got her out with the help of a large number of luckless passers-by. I had learned my lesson: a Landrover will do the impossible as long as a few of its wheels have something to grip, and to my credit it must be said that I never again got seriously stuck — apart from once later in the Sahara, but that didn't count as there was supposed to be no mud there.

The Landrover became a much-appreciated friend to whom we always referred in the feminine gender. For ten years she never let me down, first crossing Iceland, twice "doing" the Sahara, climbing mountains and crossing rivers all over Europe, and never giving up. She once caught fire, occasionally lost a few pieces, and after every mishap acquired more personality.

As the budget for the expedition was extremely limited I sought sponsorship. I managed to convince Erin Foods that it would be useful to them to have their freeze-dried products tested under sub-arctic conditions. That, of course, was a bit of an exaggeration; Icelandic summers are no colder than Irish ones. The response was more than generous, and a truckload arrived. On the premise that each of the three expedition members would consume a pack of soup a day in the cold and at least a pound of dried meat, for years after we had come back we were still eating Icelandic dinners. On Iceland itself we certainly didn't starve whatever other deprivations we suffered. Because of a friend who had a friend who knew somebody in Irish Distillers we were presented with a number of bottles of the hard stuff which was meant to strengthen the brotherhood of man if not open doors up north where licensing laws are somewhat restrictive.

So, at the beginning of June we said goodbye to wife, children and friends and set off for Scotland where we embarked on the *MV Gullfoss* which plied in those days between Leith, the harbour of Edinburgh, and Reykjavik, the capital of the Land of Ice and Fire. The team consisted of Sue, general factotum and dogsbody; Oscar who had various duties in the ornithological field; and me as leader, which meant that more often than not I had to do the cooking. In Edinburgh we dutifully visited the castle where fulmar petrels circled the ramparts; we had an animated conversation with a guard who was about seven feet tall in his bearskin, and continued to the harbour where the brand-new Landrover was hoisted upon the forecastle. We boarded hours later and in the evening we chugged out towards the Arctic Ocean. Our ship was soon surrounded by scores of fulmars and countless puffins, guillemots, gannets and storm petrels. There were bonxies galore, kittywakes and the inevitable herring gulls. The real highlights consisted of some Leach's petrels and one rare great shearwater which sent Oscar into raptures.

Susan, Oscar and the author o/b the MV Gullfoss, on their way to Iceland, watching a flock of stormy Petrels.

A pair of cranes on a lake in southern Lapland, on their way to the lonely tundra where they build their nests. They winter in northeast Africa and follow traditional routes to and from their breeding grounds. All over Europe cranes are on the decline because of the destruction of their habitats. They were abundant in Ireland during the Middle Ages but have become rare visitors since; during the autumn of 1984 seven birds stayed for a while in County Wexford.

In Ireland the heron is commonly called "crane", which can cause confusion; real cranes are much taller and feed in fields on grubs and large insects, not on fish like the common heron.

A heron, the 'Irish crane'.

WILL I OR WON'T I BLOW IT ALL ON A SMARTY?

MJOLKARÍS
ᴍᴍᴍ 900·
ᴍᴍᴍ 2 00

Icelandic Inflation

On the last day aboard the venerable *Gullfoss*, everyone was out on deck to watch the approach of the promised land, when at last through clouds and mist the outlines of the Vestmannaeyjar, the islands of the westmen appeared, and the headland of Dyrholaey on the mainland. On the outer island could be seen hundreds of nesting gannets and the ship was sailing through a cloud of Leach's petrels and the first Arctic skuas appeared, promises of things to come. Large basking sharks moved slowly to avoid the ship. Then Surtsey came into view. This small island was the latest addition among the many islands around Iceland and had only been created a couple of years before, when a volcanic eruption underwater had thrown up enough material to raise a mountain from the waves. Still smoking and devoid of vegetation it had become a centre of scientific investigation. Rarely had a similar chance to study the emergence of life on a totally sterile environment occurred.

In the early morning we docked in the harbour of Reykjavik, the car was hoisted onto the quay and after some pleasantries with the customs who argued that we couldn't bring all this food in, never mind the bottles, we were eventually allowed into the town. We decided to stay for the first

night in a real hotel as Susan had been seasick and needed nursing back to her usual cheerful self before we were to brave the inhospitable interior.

Reykjavik is not an appealing town. Half the population of Iceland is concentrated in and around the capital which still doesn't amount to much. There is an air of utility: wooden houses with tin roofs, a couple of shopping streets with banks and the post office and a restaurant with the epicurean name of Hressingarskalinn which became a favourite as it was the only place in Iceland where we were able to get a meal for less than the price of one in an expensive restaurant back in Ireland.

On our first and as it turned out most successful expedition we kept a log which was dutifully written up each day by whoever felt the urge. Icelanders get mixed up in deciding when it is time to go to bed or when to get up and we soon fell into this state of confusion. Dusk and sunrise are not there to guide one. People retire when they feel like it in summer, or stay awake for the whole season, or so it seems. We learned soon that there was nothing remarkable in going to a farm at half past three in the morning to buy eggs or milk: you'd find the children playing in the yard. Or up to a petrol pump and finding everybody fast asleep in the afternoon — which didn't matter very much as there was a tin on top of the pump to put your money in after you'd helped yourself. During an Icelandic summer one loses all sense of time, and with all that constant light also the dates get lost after a few days of thirteen hours, followed by some of twenty nine.

Sheep of the midnight sun

"What time is it?"
"Only half June yet!"

In Iceland there are few metalled roads, apart from some in and around the population centres in the south-west, and immediately after we had left Reykjavik we found ourselves on a track, the fat tyres of the landrover crunching over the broken stone. Where a track like that gets worn, it develops into a washboard of endless rows of transverse ridges which make travelling at speed one long rattle. That first day we rattled along for 350 kilometres so when we eventually pitched the tent beside a beautifully clear mountain stream which got its waters straight from a glacier, it took us some time to get accustomed again to a non-vibrating environment.

The landscape was overpowering, serene and beautiful, full of flowers and birds of all description. In a small marsh red-necked phalaropes were courting, there was a large colony of screaming Arctic terns and there were eiderduck; we had seen merlins and a peregrine falcon; we had passed through rich meadowland with black-tailed godwits

happened to be in Akureyri, Iceland's second town and as devoid of immediate charms as the capital. The festivities were about to start and we hung on. I hoped it would give us some "local colour" as an antedote to nothing but birds and volcanoes but we needn't have bothered. Modern Vikings are not as exuberant as Italians and are not inclined to dance in the street unless totally drunk — "blindfuller" as they have it, a combination of two old norse words meaning, yes, blind and full so we left at the first opportunity and filmed the flotillas of eider with their ducklings in the harbour and made for Myvatn.

Myvatn means "lake of the midges" and the name is well chosen; it is also one of the richest wildfowl lakes in the whole of northern Europe where some 15,000 duck of fifteen different species breed. The lake consists of thirty eight square kilometres of shallow water which in the long and sunny days of the subarctic summer gets quite warm. In the centre of an area of great vol-

I THINK WE'RE GETTING RAIN !

fording one of a thousand rivers —————

and redshanks and lapwings galore. As we pitched the tent and made dinner of dried meat and tinned button mushrooms, with the sun just touching the horizon, I realised that Iceland had been the best choice ever for a first expedition.

The seventeenth of June is Iceland's national holiday: on that date in 1944, the Icelandic republic had been founded after centuries of Danish domination. We

canic activity, it is surrounded by green and luscious grassland. The farmers around the lake "milk" the ducks. Eggs are taken but in each nest five or six eggs are left to produce more ducks for next year. In return the waterfowl are rigorously protected. On the houses there are nestboxes for duck, goldeneyes and others that elsewhere would breed in hollow trees.

Morocco, a land of contrasts.
In the south, in M'Hamid at the edge of the
Sahara sand dunes, a little boy running
home, a square building of sun-dried bricks,
and not a tree in sight. In the lush north of the
country, amidst wheatfields and orange
groves, cattle egrets abound. They get their
name from their habit of following cattle and
large game to prey on the insects the animals
disturb. Cattle egrets worldwide are doing
well and are spreading. Originally an Indo-
African bird, they have colonised southern
Europe, Australia and even South America.
They are sometimes seen in Ireland.

A spotted orchid

At the Northern end of Mývatn there is an official camping site which we scorned. When filming one doesn't want too many people around, chasing subjects away or poking dirty fingers in lenses.

Mývatn is rich in minerals and there is a phenomenal growth of diatoms and other algae which form the food for myriads of insects which in their turn feed the wildfowl. At the bottom of the lake there is a thick deposit of the remains of the diatoms, tiny shells of silica. That diatom-mud is extracted and further washed and refined in a large factory at the side of the lake. The factory uses enormous amounts of hot water of which there is an abundance. The lake is in the centre of a geothermal area: there are hot rivers, under and above the ground and you only have to drill a hole to get overheated steam spouting up, which

Hen ptarmigan

can be both convenient and spectacular. The refined diatom-earth is used for many purposes: as a polishing agent, as a filtering agent and for the making of dynamite.

The volcanic nature of the region is apparent all around. A few kilometres to the east there is Námaskard with solfataros, hot springs and boiling mud. Here sulphur was mined in the Middle Ages and as it is a constituent of gun-powder the area was of strategic importance and wars were fought over it.

Since my first visit to Mývatn I have been back many times but nothing could match the excitement of this first foray into the wonders of Iceland's north and the discoveries that were made. There was Grotagjá, an underground river with water of exactly 40 degrees centigrade. It runs through a fault in the lava fields and is fed from deep underground. In one spot a hole had been dynamited in the roof so that the river, if one was careful, became accessible and could be used as a local bath. There was nothing more pleasant, after a hard day's driving through the lava fields, than clambering down into the bowels of the earth and letting dirt and tiredness slowly melt away in the beautifully hot and clear water of this natural jacuzzi. There was another cave beside it which you could reach by diving through a passage; you arrived in a totally dark world of steam and wet heat smelling of sulphurated hydrogen, a perfume slightly reminiscent of rotten eggs.

Námaskard

Herđubreiđ unconquered

With Mývatn as a base we made forays into the uninhabited interior. We had been lucky enough to come across Nick, an American student who was conducting a study of gyr falcons, the pride of Iceland's birds of prey. The four of us set off one day, first east through the smoking moonscapes of Námaskard and then to the Jøkelsá ni Fullum, a huge river that flows from the glacier on top of Askja, a huge volcano in the centre of the central desert. The track lead first along a number of extinct volcanoes through empty lava desert with an oasis of greenery here and there; later it met a vast field of block lava, terrible and terrifying stuff which looked like solidified black porridge cooked for giants. Herđubreiđ, the solitary extinct volcano from which it all had come, stands in majesty in the middle of the great desert of the central highlands. In the clean and dry air it was already visible on the horizon from fifty miles away. It was impossible not to fall in love with it at first sight, though it was hard to get to know the object of our affection. When at last we had reached what we thought was a point near enough to walk up to the lady of the highlands, bedecked with a small white glacier as a crown with a cloud as trail, we

discovered that we had to cross rivers and an outsize moat of impassible screes made out of the most unsympathetic lumps of lava. Iceland is a boon for lay geologists like me: whereas in Ireland you have an embarrassing choice of stone with long names to contend with, on Iceland everything you meet you may safely call 'lava', from the floating pumice to the volcanic glass called obsidian, but all is lava. Even Icelandic beaches are made of grainy forms of the rotten stuff. Of course, real geologists know better: they talk about tephra and ropy lava, bombs and a whole list of Italian names.

According to our map the mountain was only six kilometres away but we were defeated by the sheer size of it. We easily discovered the nests of a few pink-feeted geese. Lava is full of minerals and potentially fertile; one element, nitrogen, is missing but that can be supplied by bird droppings, making a goose nest stand out as a small green bump in the middle of desolation.

Around Herđubreiđ was a network of very shallow and wide but fast-flowing rivers and a system of small lakes and some beautiful marshes with lush grass and yellow-green sphagnum and a choice of flowers. These were an oasis in the middle

A sure sign of autumn approaching: a curlew feather on the beach.

A hoverfly (Syrphus) feeding in a poppy in the garden.

no parking?

Like anywhere else on Iceland in scenic spots there were a couple of spotless toilets; there was also a camping site surrounded by rubbish bins and a mountain hut which one could use during inclement weather. This was beautifully furnished and fully equipped with a stove with cut wood already inside, Primus stoves and paraffin oil, a supply of emergency food, bunks and mattresses but no caretaker. On the inside of the door was a box where one was asked to pay a charge.

From Herðubreið the track wound its way again southwards through lava of all sizes and shapes — ashes, pebbles, sand and block lava. Often it was possible to travel at speed, freewheeling through the bends of the track, but mostly it was slow going through the petrified porridge. Then one of us would drive the car while the others took shortcuts over the block lava and looked for flowers and lichens in the hope too of raising the snowy owl which was said to breed in these parts. The trip through this totally unspoiled, new and original landscape was exhilarating, light clouds and wind making the scenery change from minute to minute.

Passing rows of smaller mountains, at last Askja loomed on the horizon — the biggest complex of volcanoes in the very centre of Iceland and without difficulty we reached its foot. We stayed the night at the foot of the mountain and returned the following day. Beside the main track we had found the nest of a raven and one of a gyr falcon with three young. We had climbed up

of the bare and black desolation where only here and there tufts of wispy grass and lichens provided some colour. Tall angelica towered here among the streams; dwarf willow and Arctic birch on which the ptarmigan fed provided all in the way of trees. Many of them were of a very respectable age but because of the snows in winter grew no higher than a foot or so. It was hard to believe that the gnarled horizontal stems were in reality the trunks of ancient real trees. In the oasis there were also many birds: whooper swans which in Ireland we only meet in winter; mergansers courting on the little lakes; trusting red-necked phalaropes, snow buntings and white wagtails.

Herðubreið, here we come

on the way to Askja

to the nest to see how many young falcons there were, had stayed very briefly so as not to disturb the birds and later had the satisfaction of seeing the young being fed by the female. We had filmed the scene from below with a telephoto lens. We had found too that somebody had set up a hide rather close to the nest; we had taken this hide down and left it with a note, pointing out that setting up a hide so close to a gyr's nest was illegal.

On the way back home, in quite a jubilant mood after all the marvellous things we had seen, we found that the nest had been abandoned and that the three young had either starved to death or had succumbed to disease. Nick who had been studying gyr falcons for a long time had various theories but none satisfactorily explained the death of the whole brood. As we all felt partly responsible for this tragedy the trip back over Mývatnheiði was a gloomy one. Moreover we had been travelling the whole day by now through demanding terrain and, now far past midnight, everybody was dead beat. Even the customary visit to the hole to wash off three days of driving in hot mineral waters did nothing to cheer us up. At around six in the morning we had supper and slept. It took another week or so before we were back to a normal schedule and before the sight of those three dead tiercels had faded.

In the meantime we had acquired neighbours at our camp along the lake. A contingent from the British Army had arrived on a kind of adventure course which to me seemed more of holiday than serious soldiering. A couple of jolly chaps were under the command of an even jollier lieutenant who spent his days fishing very successfully in the lake. Practically every evening when we returned from yet another brilliant tour into the interior, resulting in even more close-ups of whimbrels, harlequin ducks and what-have-you, we would find a couple of mighty char, salmon-like fish in which the lake abounded, shoved under our tent. Relationships between our two camps blossomed to such an extent that they were flying our Irish tricolour and we had a Union Jack in the shape of a shopping bag acquired in Edinburgh fluttering from our washing line.

golden plover

We made a trip to the Arctic Ocean, driving east towards the river which we then followed to the sea over the very largest farm in the whole of Europe. Iceland is strong in big features and the farm is larger than the whole duchy of Luxemburg, though there is more grass in one single meadow in Luxemburg than on this entire, enormous farm.

Wildlife laws are very strict in Iceland and an example to other European countries. All birds are protected but time-honoured ways of exploiting them continue. Eiderduck are farmed for their down and are strictly preserved. Their nesting islands are shielded from predators such as skuas — gull-like robbers — and each island is provided with small flags on long poles which the duck don't mind but the skuas dislike. When the breeding season is over the down that lined the nests is gathered, cleaned and washed and used for the making of eiderdowns, sleeping bags and the lining of coats.

Great care is taken to keep the areas free of predators though some of these are afforded even stronger protection. It is illegal to go closer than three-hundred metres from a known gyr falcon's nest. They are mighty birds of prey much beloved by falconers and they fetch many thousands of pounds on the black market. We had thought gyrs to be very rare but around Mývatn alone there were eleven occupied eyries that year, which for a big bird of prey represents a remarkable density.

The largest of the Icelandic raptors, the white-tailed eagle, survives only in very small numbers, but the very rarest bird in Iceland is the little auk, a truly arctic sea-bird. It only breeds in one or two pairs on a small island called Grisey.

fulmar petrel

little auk

With Iceland's large fishing industry it had been thought a good idea to introduce and farm mink for the fur trade, feeding the animals on side products of the fishing industry. The inevitable happened: mink escaped and in the large and empty country established themselves in no time, reverting in the process to their original colour, black. A gyr falcon will feed on one species of bird only. Mink however, will kill anything that comes their way, be it duck on their nest, young of waterfowl, waterhens, songbirds, fish, mice or other rodents. Moreover mink are prolific breeders and when food supply is plentiful and there are no natural enemies they soon become a real threat to the existing order. A number of hunters are employed full-time to contain their numbers but their task is hopeless in an empty country one and a half times the size of Ireland.

49

On Iceland there seemed to be quite a healthy ecology; there were plenty of predators, indicating that there were also plenty of birds to feed on. The relationship between predators and prey is often misunderstood. It is not the number of predators that decides the density of prey animals, it is the other way round. If in an area you find a great number of, for example, sparrowhawks you may be sure that the density of small birds on which they feed is also great. Only in rare cases, usually after the introduction of animals that are not native to the area, is there trouble. More often than not, of course, it is humans that are the cause of the trouble.

One delight we discovered in the sub-arctic was the general tameness of birds and animals which was also, of course, very convenient if we wanted to photograph or paint them. There was this woodmouse residing in a stone wall against which we were having lunch at two in the morning in sunlight. Attracted by the smell of Erin soup and Skyr — the Icelandic form of yoghurt which is addictive after you've got used to its consistency — the mouse came out and more or less asked to be fed, taking crumbs out of Sue's hand without much hesitation. Oscar was in continuous raptures, wading through shallow pools with phalaropes around his feet.

One day we saw a whooper swan sitting on its nest at some distance and we slowly crept up to it in order to take snaps. We needn't have bothered getting wet knees. When at last we reached her we had to lift her bodily off the nest to see how many eggs she had, while the cob was feeding undisturbed nearby. Another illusion shattered: real wild swans, the Children of Lir, behaving no differently from the kitchen or garden mute swans which had bred around my ancestral home in Rotterdam's city park.

Iceland has a few specialities in the waterfowl line. One of them is the harlequin duck, a cute little fellow of American ancestry. These duck are to be found on fast-flowing rivers only and a favourite and well-known spot to watch them is where the Laxá flows from Mývatn. They got a lot of attention from every birdwatcher who ever turns up in Iceland and maybe they were used to visitors. Anyhow, there they were,

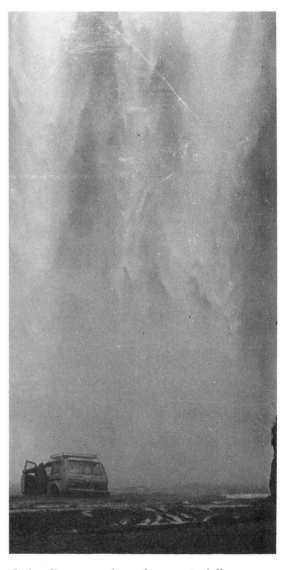

Icelandic car-wash: under a waterfall.

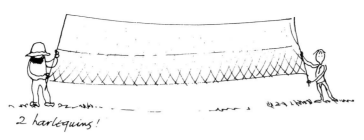

2 harlequins!

one pair fast asleep in the grass, speckled with buttercups at the opposite bank of the river, only acknowledging our arrival with a wink. Filming sleeping birds eventually becomes boring; we wanted them on the water, doing their thing which is racing upstream, diving, courting, mating maybe, laying eggs. It took quite a few stones thrown into the river to make them wake up and start performing for the benefit of viewers at home. In every birdwatcher a primitive hunter slumbers and the thought crept up that it would be quite exciting to catch one and have it in the hand for closer examination. There was a conveniently high bridge over the Laxá from which we hung down a wadernet, a sturdier edition of the mistnet. Within five minutes they had flown into our trap, been examined, photographed for posterity and, of course, released straight away. Mind you, the whole exercise had been illegal as only qualified Icelanders were allowed to catch birds for scientific purposes.

harlequin ♂

There was more to Iceland than the delights of Mývatn and we made long expeditions to the coast and into the interior. One day, passing a small, drunken sign marked Dettifoss, which pointed towards a side-track, we came upon the biggest waterfall in Europe where some six million litres of glacier water fall into a gorge every second, a truly awe-inspiring and roaring spectacle. We tried to film it but I must confess that I could find no way to compress all these tonnes of descending water onto a 16mm frame. There was no way I could even give an approximation, though I did my best with zooms and pans and all the tricks of the trade. I was encountering the restriction every film maker has, the difficulty of relating size of picture to reality. Filming small birds in close up works fine; extremely small living creatures very much enlarged onto a screen works even better. But to give a true impression of a larger natural phenomenon, of the extent and sound of Dettifoss, where there is nothing to give a true scale, is impossible and one has to live with that.

On the whole we had been lucky with the weather. There is a proverb in the land of ice and fire that, if you don't like the weather, you have only to wait five minutes as it is sure to change. The large central desert works as a barrier between two climatic zones; if it rains in the north one can be certain that there is sun in the south and vice versa. So, when we ran into a couple of days of wet weather we crossed the island again and tried our luck in the south.

We knew that there would be a yearly horse show in a village on the south coast called Hella, but we arrived to a continuous downpour which lasted a full three days. Thousands of very wet horses had gathered with their riders from all over Iceland, some having travelled for many days to get there, camping along the way. The size of the average Icelander and that of his horse are

hella campsite

about the same and the equine part of the combination is the more elegant. On the camping site we discovered that the most popular horse was the white one which comes in a bottle, it was used by everyone to dry out their cockles. The Icelandic horse, though, is something else again. It is descended from the horses that were brought during the Middle Ages by the Vikings on their longboats and the race of small sturdy animals has not changed since. They are the same as the old Greek ones on the Elgin marbles from the Parthenon in Athens. In the past they were used for transport and farm work and left to fend for

themselves in the open, even through the winter. Nowadays tractors and four-wheel-drive cars have taken over and keeping horses in Iceland has become a sport and a hobby as elsewhere in Europe. Horsetrekking through the interior in summer is now a popular outdoor sport — an undertaking in which one rider needs a number of horses to carry provisions and camping gear. In Germany and the Netherlands the keeping of Icelandic horses has become fashionable with people who can pay for it and a considerable export business of horses from Iceland has developed.

In Hella in the rain we had our work cut out, filming horses standing, eating, being ridden and groomed, scratching, rolling about, rearing, running and walking; horses

of every colour imaginable; never had we seen so many horses. In the refreshment tent huge farmers who had come from lonely homesteads in the interior were carving away with their pocket knives at the limitless supply of smoked sheep heads, one of the more visually revolting dishes of the Icelandic kitchen but very sustaining and tasty.

The horses have a remarkable way of covering ground, a special extra step called the "skeid" whereby the horse and its rider manage to keep horizontally in a straight line. Not being a horseman myself I can't give a more technical explanation. In vain we tried to persuade some of the least drunken riders to let us have a go on their mounts but as the prerequisite of riding turned out to be the possession of a saddle, which we had forgotten to pack into the car when leaving Dublin, we didn't get very far. When everybody on the campsite was more or less asleep we sneaked to a paddock and talked to some individual horses who didn't seem to have any objection and we skeided saddleless round the field without, to our great surprise, falling off.

After the exciting but wet days in Hella we continued eastward along the south coast where there was a vast wide plain between the cliffs and the sea. Here plentiful fulmar petrels, which are cliff-breeders, had their single eggs on ledges far inland. As they are curious birds, as soon as we stopped the car and walked up to the cliff the birds came down and circled round. Of course, any Irish fulmar will do the same thing, greeting you on your arrival and watching you in a most sympathetic way with one big black eye. The most beautiful sight I remember was that of a family of whoopers flying along the cliff, sharply silhouetted in the low light, but before we could stop and get the camera out they had gone.

Vatnajøkull is the biggest glacier in Europe and is larger than all the others combined. We were happy to discover that a track went straight up to a smaller lump of ice, called Solheimajøkull — the glacier of the house of the sun. It looked formidable, when we stood at an arête and looked down into its blue crevasses; it was just as in the textbooks: an outlet glacier draining an icecap, the pressure of which pushes the ice down to a lower level where it melts until an equilibrium is reached between melting and the advance of the ice. Where the ice mass passed over uneven bedrock crevasses had developed. The ice had first been snow or hail that had fallen many years ago higher up, had possibly melted in the sunshine and refrozen again many times during the nights. It had become first granular and later harder and more solid and the mass of it was now slowly descending to sea level.

As the weather was fine we decided to try to conquer Solheimajøkull, which was a rather stupid notion to put it mildly. Just getting to the foot of the glacier was difficult enough as we waded through shallow streams of icy water, sank into quicksands and got stuck at a moat where the water rushed out from underneath the ice. We managed, though, and started our ascent. On an average of one in every five years there is a volcanic eruption on Iceland which throws no mean amount of volcanic ash — tephra — into the air. When that lands on top of a glacier the black stuff collects more heat from the sun than the ice itself, the ice underneath melts faster and the tephra collects in pointed heaps.

We had neither icepicks nor proper shoes and when higher up we looked down into the blue crevasses and realised that if any of us slipped and fell into the heart of the glacier the only way we would get out again would be deep-frozen. After a couple of hours we had had enough and very carefully indeed made our way back to safety without mishap, which was more due to luck than anything else.

Red throated diver on nest

Near the foot of the glacier was a small lake caused by the retreating ice which housed a pair of red-throated divers, very common birds in Iceland which also breed in very small numbers in Ireland. We had no trouble finding the nest and spent the rest of the day watching and filming the birds greeting and courting, and enjoying the elegance of their demeanour. Once again they were exceedingly tame and didn't mind us at all.

arctic skua

On the plain between the coastal cliff and the sea masses of birds were breeding: arctic skuas and gulls, mergansers, greylag geese and a choice of waders, the magnificent golden plovers, whimbrels and redshanks. The sky was full of their cries and calls and the songs of smaller birds, white

wagtails, skylarks and snow buntings. We were struck by an intriguing thought: that whooper sitting so unconcerned on her eggs at the edge of an Icelandic lake, would we meet her again in Ireland? The chances were we would. And later, during the winter when I was filming whoopers on a pond in Arklow I had the notion that I had met two of the flock before and that I had seen their three young in the shape of eggs even though there had been five at the time we had lifted the mother off her nest. It was a fanciful but not impossible notion, and certainly after Iceland I looked at wild swans with different eyes.

grey seals were playing, the whole scene familiar to anyone who has been on any bird cliff anywhere in the north Atlantic. Out at sea gannets, which have huge and expanding colonies on islands around the coast, were diving.

Puffins are caught by nets, plucked from the sky as they wheel past. In the past it was from sheer necessity that birds were harvested but now it is only a sport and the numbers that can be taken are severely restricted. When the young birds are fledged many get lost over the township and land in the streets. They are carefully collected and then near the town are released by being thrown out over sea.

Dyrholaey

Eventually we ended up at Dyrholaeye — Portland in English — the most southerly point of mainland Iceland which stood out on the lava beach like an island. It was the first point we had seen on our arrival nearly a month earlier and it was fitting that as we stood there we saw the old *Gullfoss* steaming up to Reykjavik. We used the occasion to film the ship from high above and later cut the shot into my first programme about Iceland, combined with shots taken on our arrival at Dyrholaeye as seen from the ship. Such are the tricks of film making, compressing a whole month into a couple of seconds and getting away with it.

Dyrholaeye means the "island with the hole like a door" which is rather apt and its steep cliffs house innumerable seabirds, mainly kittywakes and auks of which the puffins are the most numerous. In the surf

netting of puffins

Our time in Iceland was up; all the film had been exposed and we returned reluctantly to Reykjavik. Once again the trusty Landrover was hoisted aboard and two days later we would again go to bed when it was really dark and not only our watch said that it was time to retire.

On the trip back to Scotland we rediscovered the softness of mattresses after all the hard lava we had endured, and as we drove back through Scotland we enjoyed the forgotten sensation of seeing real trees of well over eight feet high.

Arctic tern

Merlin van Gelderen

Sahara

IT WAS more or less natural that after having travelled through the Icelandic wastes I should try to see desert of a different sort. In my youth, during a stint as a sailor, I had been to Indonesia and returning via the Suez Canal had had a few days to spare when the ship was on the quay in Suez. With some friends we had rented a taxi and gone to Cairo to see the pyramids. There's a lot of sand and stones between Suez and Cairo so I had some experience of desert. During my hitch-hiking days too I had ventured into the south of Tunisia and seen a tantalising glimpse of the real thing, the Sahara, the largest desert in the world, and it had given me a taste for more.

We set off in early spring, carrying an incongruous plastic dinghy on top of the landrover, down through Spain, a delight in itself. The easiest and cheapest way to get into Africa is the ferry from Algeciras in the south to Ceuta — Bab Septa in Arabic — at the other side. As companion I had an American student, Johnny, who was at a loose end and a film-buff to boot. He was good though sometimes bewildered company. The idea was to drive down via the Atlas mountains and from there to play it by ear, filming as we went. The last night in Europe we camped at the beach at Tarifa looking at birds and the lights of Tangiers in the promised land, until we were arrested by a couple of Franco's soldiers, who luckily didn't discover that we had a car full of cameras. They let us go after some arguments, extremely servile from our side. Apparently we had driven straight through barbed wire into a military zone, which is easily enough performed in a landrover.

Morocco turned out to be more friendly. It was early spring and the north was still cold and partly flooded. The country was full of large flocks of storks. Crossing the Strait of Gibraltar we had already filmed enormous numbers of birds of prey that use the narrow stretch of sea to soar from Africa where they winter to spread out again all over Europe. It was a fantastic sight to see a flock of 300 buzzards and countless smaller birds of prey; we had arrived at just the right time.

In the North of Morocco is an area comparatively unknown to holidaymakers and as wild, or even wilder than anywhere else in this large and varied region of the Rif mountains where one travels over narrow roads which lead over rough passes with mediaeval-looking villages hidden deep in steep valleys. Geologically and also historically this area is the same as Andalucia, and more Mediterranean than African.

Merdja Zerga, in Morocco's north-west, is an area of lakes surrounded by marshes, which is famous for its waterfowl. It is here that many European duck spend the winter and masses of waders pass through in spring and autumn. The area is not only popular with bird-watchers but also with hunters. We stayed there for a couple of days, trying in vain to get near the lake itself through land where one needed more than a landrover. Our nights were filled with the calls of waders and though we could only guess at their numbers, without ever getting close enough to film, there were enough locals to keep us happy. We zigzagged further through the plains in the north until at last we reached Marrakech, the pearl of the south, after a memorable couple of days at Mechrâ-Bennabou halfway between Casablanca and Marrakech, where a large artificial lake in the Oued Oum Rbia, the Rbia river, turned out to be an ornithological paradise. By then we had become thoroughly used to Moroccan ways which, after all, are not all that different from those of Ireland.

We had found a friend in a local boy who travelled on with us and was a deft hand at catching things, from lizards to snakes and mice. He also did the shopping and it turned out that with him about we could easily halve our grocery bills. In Morocco as anywhere else there is a different scale of prices for tourists; to be in with the locals can make a serious difference in the budget.

It was fascinating to learn from him about farming and the way of life in that part of the country. Mohammed's father was employed by the Ministry of Forestry which was busy reafforesting the eroded hill-sides, bare as a result of many centuries of cutting, neglect and over-grazing. In many parts this is a hopeless task as the soil, impoverished through wind and water has become totally devoid of any plant cover. The hills are contoured so as to catch as much rain as possible before it runs down and away into the wadis, the seasonal rivers. The main trees planted are eucalyptus and aleppo pines, both of which thrive under difficult conditions. The eucalyptus is fast growing and provides timber for building and charcoal for cooking.

At the lake we had made a deal involving a bottle of wine with the local police who let us camp in the forest on state ground. There we entertained and were entertained at night by the local youths who had spent the day looking after the roaming herds of sheep and goats, all of them eager to show off the French they had learned at school, reciting fables of La Fontaine into "la machine", the tape-recorder which was an endless source of amusement until we ran out of batteries. There was a seventeen-year-old who made a violin — a rebaba — out of an empty half-gallon oil tin with the strands of the clutch cable of a motor-bike as strings. He would sing endless ballads in a falsetto-voice, accompanying himself on his metal handywork. As he had the other

monitor lizard

a bulbul

bird's call-note; a swallow "tifliliss", and a raven "chraab" in Arabic and "ah'akar" in local Berber. We learned fast, and we also learned that in Morocco five languages are spoken: Arabic, two Berber languages with an endless number of dialects, French which is taught in school, and Spanish in the north.

On the west coast of Morocco where the Atlas mountains go down to the sea we were camped on the widest, emptiest and most delightful beach in all Africa — at least in the Africa I have seen — with huge Atlantic rollers coming in, the same as those in County Donegal but somewhat warmer. Nearby was a village, Asni, where we did our shopping. One day we wanted eggs for which I hadn't the Arabic handy, nor were they in sight. The shop was run by an enormously fat man who spent his days crocheting dainty skullcaps. I could not get across that it was eggs we wanted and eventually had to resort to giving an imitation of a cackling hen. It made the shopkeeper's day and added to the mirth of the rest of the village's inhabitants who all roared with laughter, making me feel extremely sheepish. We got our eggs though.

boys in stitches most of the time I have no doubt that his songs couldn't stand translating.

We had with us a fat book on the birds of North Africa and were anxious to learn the local names. The boys who tramped the fields with their flocks all day were splendid naturalists and more than obliging in telling us bird names, either in Arabic or in Berber, when we showed them the pictures. We would then laboriously and phonetically write the names down. There are sounds in Arabic which are impossible to put on paper if you don't know the language. But I'm still proud to remember that a hoopoe is "hood-hood", easy to remember for that is the

asni

'hood-hood'

A year later, passing again through the same village, I popped in to say hello — "salem aleikum". There was the same man again, still fat and still crocheting a skullcap. He gave a big grin and then an uncontrollable outburst of laughter which brought in the rest of the village again, all cackling like mad and trying (in vain) to imitate my Dutch accent. It ended in a party with tea and sweets and we left with six eggs as a present.

It still was spring and there was snow on the peaks of the Atlas mountains, the 2650 metres of Oukaimeden glistening in the sunshine. The skiing season was about finished but the cablecar was still working so we rented a pair of skis between us and ascended to see Morocco from the top, while alpine choughs circled around us. That night, with sore muscles in places where we should have none we camped at the edge of a snow field and discovered that there are scorpions at such heights as well as a choice of the finest alpine plants. Morocco turned out to be full of surprises.

At the bottom of the mountain lay a small village, Imlil, from which climbing expeditions departed. There wasn't a horizontal two square metres in the place to pitch a tent without flattening the crops of thin barley so we ended up being guests of Tansin, the local guide and mountaineer who ran a kind of simple hostel. Imlil was, and hopefully still is, a remarkable place, nestling at the bottom of a deep valley at the end of a long and narrow gorge. Although isolated it still had an international atmosphere about it, with plaques and mementos of many mountaineering clubs and a guestbook with famous names.

The Berber village itself was as primitive and friendly as could be. In the narrow fields, often only a few metres square, crops were grown and we were shown the water-powered mill where a small girl sat all day, feeding handfuls of barley into the topstone

of the mill worked by an overshot water-wheel. On the slopes boys herded goats and sent down into the valley the mixed music of reed-flute and ceaseless bleating, now and then added to by a clatter of stones. It was the most peaceful village and our filming was an intrusion. But life was not as idyllic as it seemed. Any medical services lay six hours' walk away. Tansin showed us what he had for emergencies: a few bandages, a half-empty tube of aspirin and a bottle of disinfectant; for the rest of their medical supplies the village depended on casual visitors.

Hospitality was total. We were fed and given presents and treated like royalty, and there was little we could do in return. During the weeks that we travelled the Moroccan highways and byways we were to experience time and again the graceful and natural hospitality of a friendly people who took our — to them sometimes outlandish — behaviour and appearance in their stride.

One night, climbing up to a bare plateau, we noticed a sign at the beginning of a very rough trail that mentioned an Arabic place-name which was ten kilometres away. Following the trail that wound through the most moon-like of bare landscapes we eventually reached a tiny village on the banks of a river where we were met by the schoolteacher who somehow knew that we were coming though we had not seen anybody all the way over the rocks and through the wadis. We were ceremoniously given a bit of sandbank to camp on and a bucket of couscous and salad after a tour along the houses to shake hands with every villager in sight. We were the first car to make it to the place for six years, we were told, and we were made more than welcome, with marhabas all around. Our popularity rose again when we gave all the youngsters of the village, many of whom had never seen a car before, a ride on top of the bonnet and the roof. After that we were showered with mishmish, apricots and other fruits of the gardens along the river and after an im-promptu concert with drums and flutes it was rather late before we went to bed, with a candle stuck in the sand in front of the tent around which a fearful looking camel-spider was chasing the moths the candle-light ex-tracted from a velvet desert night. No sky so dark as a Sahara night and no star so bright.

camel-spider or solfugid

The high Atlas is rather devoid of vegetation apart from low scrub in the valleys and some tenacious trees-of-life hanging onto the slopes and a few new plantations. The mountains had formerly been heavily wooded with cedars and other trees but now only forests of holm oaks still cover many of the lower slopes. We found surprises at each bend of the road: a choice of butterflies, chameleons and other lizards, enormous bush crickets and grasshoppers and not a few birds most of which were rather familiar, including huge flocks of house-sparrows wherever there was wheat.

The highest pass, the Tizi-n-test was breathtaking, at a height of 2100 metres. After that we slowly descended into the lowlands again, feeling at last that we had really arrived in Africa. We explored the southern half of Morocco and made it to Ouarzazate from where a track led straight through real sand dunes to M'hamid at the edge of the Sahara proper, at least and at last looking what a desert should, with endless sands, fierce-looking tribesmen riding camels and picture-book oases with date palms.

The general idea that the Sahara is an empty space devoid of life, monotonous and composed of sand into which never a drop of rain falls is a wrong one. The Sahara certainly is vast, more than three and a half million square miles of North Africa, larger than all of the United States, but barely 15 per cent of its surface is covered in sand. There are mountains 10,000 feet high, it has a lake in the Chad, larger than any in Europe, and, if anything, it is overpopulated. There are too many people grazing too many sheep and goats.

Deserts are, geologically speaking, relatively recent formations on the face of the earth, and desertification is going on at an accelerated rate, partly as a result of the

HOW A DESERT MAY BE CREATED BY MAN AND HIS BEASTS

1 ORIGINAL LANDSCAPE: WOODED HILLS AND VALLEYS WHERE THE RICH SOIL HOLDS WATER AND SO PREVENTS EROSION.

2 MAN MOVES IN: THE VALLEY IS NOW UNDER CROPS AND TIMBER IS CUT ON THE HILLS, OPENING UP THE SOIL TO WIND AND WATER.

3 THE FERTILITY OF THE FLAT LAND REDUCED: CATTLE MOVE IN AND FARMS NOW CULTIVATE THE SLOPES, ERODING THE TOPSOIL.

4 THE VALLEYS ARE EXHAUSTED, ONLY GOOD ENOUGH FOR GOATS. THE HILLS ARE LOSING MORE TOPSOIL. RAINWATER IS NOT RETAINED ANY MORE.

5 THE LANDSCAPE IS NOW BARREN AND TOTALLY FINISHED OFF BY SHEEP AND GOATS WHO REMOVE REMNANTS OF VEGETATION.

6 ALL TOPSOIL HAS DISAPPEARED. THE RIVER HAS BECOME SEASONAL BUT STILL CARRYING AWAY MATERIAL. THE LAND NO LONGER SUPPORTS LIFE.

actions of humans. Mountains have been denuded of tree-cover by cutting and burning. These first turned into grassland on which cattle could graze and when the land became poorer and poorer it was taken over by sheep and goats which are too-efficient grazers. Goats literally devour a landscape by pulling vegetation up by the roots and eating plants most other animals would leave standing. Goats can also climb quite well and will attack trees in a way cows and sheep can't. Wind and water get a grip on the topsoil which eventually is blown and washed away, down through the seasonal rivers ending up in the sea. Bare ground doesn't hold water, forest and soil does. This, of course, is not the main reason why the desert is there and spreading. The climate has been slowly changing over the centuries and the works of man are no more than marginal though he seems to do his best and nowhere more so than at the edges of the Sahara.

In some areas of Southern Morocco large stretches of land are fenced for forestation so that livestock cannot enter. The contrast is remarkable. On the outside bare and sparse vegetation, inside nothing comparable to an Irish meadow but at least there are shrubs and high grasses and a profusion of flowers after the rains in spring. It is, of course, impossible to fence off all areas capable of producing vegetation. People have to live even if in a day one sheep may further denude half an acre of soil and to provide a meal the women have to clear a quarter of an acre of dry bush to make a fire.

The problem of desertification is not exclusively an African one. Land can become dustbowls even in temperate zones with far higher rainfall when too much is asked from the soil, when too little is given back and too many ditches and hedgerows are destroyed to make agriculture more mechanised and profitable; when forests have been cleared to make grassland or endless wheatfields that lie fallow half the year to be attacked by eroding wind and rain. The whole of North Africe was once Rome's bread basket. In the mountains of the Sahara are ancient rock carvings depicting giraffes and hippopotami, ostriches and long-horned cattle, all of which have long disappeared from the scene.

Filming in a country like Morocco has its problems. Firstly there is the heat. Exposed film deteriorates fast: if it has been rattling around in a hot car for weeks on end funny things start to happen and a black camera standing in the sun becomes too hot to touch. Wildlife disappears in the middle of the day and birds fly around with their beaks wide open. That looks all right in the desert itself but rather strange on a television screen. In strict Muslim countries — and Morocco certainly is one, much more so than free-wheeling, and modern Tunisia — one does not film people, at least not without asking. If permission is given you end up with stilted shots, military salutes and passport photographs. Aiming a lens at a woman, be she eight or eighty, asked or unasked, may incur the wrath of father, husband or son, which may sometimes be soothed on a commercial basis. Cameras really spoil everything.

Once beside a waterhole in the Algerian desert we met a group of wildly dressed and beautiful tribesmen with their camels. Permission to take photographs, after some introductory polite conversation, was graciously given whereupon they neatly lined up to stare expectantly at the camera as if it were an instamatic. Only when, after much shaking of hands and blessings, the band departed I got my chance with a tele lens before they disappeared round the bend of the wadi in front of their stoic camels, burnouses swinging and no doubt discussing the strange ways of ignorant foreigners. It may not have been polite but the best shots I took were usually the result of a long lens aimed 500 yards away from a well where the local women were gathered to get water and have a spot of gossip. And I recall the beach at Agadir where I sneakily filmed a family from the back of the car, the father enjoying himself with the kids in the water and the mother, veiled and dressed in a black tent, didn't get as much as her feet wet on the hottest of days.

Children are usually more than co-operative and often you end up with a boy doing the camera-work for you so that you can be in the picture as well. In the beginning they all want to have a peep through the viewfinder and then express amazement that everything they see is in colour. Then they discover which button to press and as film is an expensive commodity you quickly disconnect the battery but they soon find out about that as well.

Once, meeting a man and his son and a herd of camels, after joining them for a meal of lovely bread and delicious sour camel's milk out of a gruesome leather bag, my host tried to invent some interesting shots for me. We decided we'd shear a camel who was under loud protest wrestled to the ground to be undone of some of its sparse wool. I couldn't have organised the whole thing better myself. Then we got a demonstration of saddling and mounting. I ended up carrying a load of wool, a goat and half a ton of firewood in the car up to the tent, miles away, the goat on top. Arriving home we were further entertained with tea and bagpipe music. Even if you can't stand the heat, the desert is the place to be, far from Torremelinos, or even Dallas for that matter.

M'hamid is at the end of the main track after crossing the Atlas mountains. From there one can continue over desert tracks further south into the great wilderness. Arriving there we became the hub of social flurry. It was the middle of the day and anybody who had nothing else to do was splashing about in a shallow pool fed by an irrigation pump. The temperature was in the 40s. We joined the crowd and in quick succession were invited for meals and parties by all the notables of the township. As he had been first we accepted the invitation of the local schoolteacher who, with a college friend, owned one of the small houses made of clay bricks. It was surprisingly cool inside, a relief after the glaring heat of the oven outside.

As the school was on holidays, the two friends had time to spare and in no time at all we had organised a trip to a mysterious lake called Irikiri. According to some people in the swimming pool there were pink long-legged birds around that could only be flamingos and it was an intriguing thought that we might see these in the middle of the desert.

We set off before sunrise, first knocking the shopkeeper out of bed to take on victuals and water and were on our way. Sunrise in the desert is spectacular and very rapid but not an hour later you wish you'd never seen it as the temperature rises steadily. You drive with everything open so as to catch as much wind as possible. You're sitting in a puddle of sweat and to replenish that you have to drink constantly. For every day you travel you take on five litres of water per head and double that to be on the safe side. Not all water in the Sahara would be considered drinkable in Ireland. There are wells with salty water, with borax and with a taste of washing soda. Each time you meet a well — they're all marked on the map with the depth and quality of the water — you try it out and if it's better than the stuff you have in the barrel in the back of the car you change it. Water is free but you have to bring your own bucket and rope. Sometimes in villages you can buy water that has been brought by tanker.

a 'dob' or euromastix

There were no oases between M'hamid and Lac Irikiri and we were entirely on our own. The ghost of a track wound laboriously in and out of wadis and between rocks and after a couple of hours it felt as if my skeleton was reduced to a bag of loose change. Of wildlife there was little, at least visible.

white-crowned black wheatear

Now and then we met a euromastix, or spiny-tailed lizard, which the Arabs call "dob": a strange miniature pre-historic monster with an extraordinary tail and a head like that of a prize-fighter; for all its fierce appearance it is mainly a vegetarian.

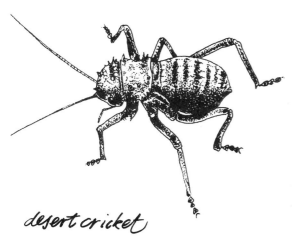

desert cricket

Birds were few and far between; there were wheatears which looked like ordinary Irish wheatears but were black all over except for a white crown in the males and, like all wheatears, a flashing white rump. Most bird-life centred around oases and settlements, where the water was. Our schoolteacher had a pair nesting in the wall of the house and they would come inside looking for scraps.

It still was early spring and flocks of swallows were on the move, sweeping low and fast over the hot ground on their way north towards the more hospitable Mediterranean and then on across to maybe nest again under the rafters of an Irish outhouse. They feed as they go and like to dash along in the lee of herds of goats and sheep and snatch up flies disturbed by the animals. They will also enter villages where boys try to hit them with stones as a sport: a strange form of welcome, but they rarely score a direct hit. It is estimated that over half of all swallows that undertake the twice-yearly crossing of the Sahara on their way between Europe and South Africa succumb to the rigours of the desert. In oases we met them drinking eagerly in puddles and at night whole flocks came to roost in the palm trees.

There were local birds as well, dusky-headed bulbuls, which no boy would dare to aim a stone at as they are held in as great esteem as the nightingales of the east. We met with many familiar birds: chiffchaffs and willow warblers, whitethroats and redstarts, all having spent the winter among the dates, the beans and pomegranate trees. An odd and very common bird in townships

was the house bunting which replaces the sparrow in the most arid of environments. Out in the open desert were fewer species: a collection of different larks and also birds of prey of which the short-toed or serpent eagle was the most common. It lives on snakes and lizards and of those there is no shortage. Wherever there was a bush of any size we could find a pair of great grey shrikes, much paler than the European ones. They also live on lizards and large insects which they impale on thorn bushes to save them for a rainy day, which is an odd expression to use in a landscape where there is but a shower every third year or so.

We observed strange phenomena in the desert. Clouds gathered and we hoped for a soft, wet day. It never came. Rain fell all right but it had evaporated before reaching the ground. Occasionally it really rains, and then the heavens truly open. One day we were camped beside an acacia tree and some bushes. (You never sleep *under* an acacia for the ground is littered with the sharpest and longest of thorns that will go straight through a car tyre, never mind a sleeping bag.) We were lying in the tent, listening to the radio which told us the news that Bobby Kennedy had been shot. The next moment there was an enormous thunderclap as a last farewell and then the skies opened up the warm water taps. In no time we were awash in swirling waters and fled to higher ground while tons of mud swept past us through the wadi. The only ones who seemed to enjoy the experience were a family of drenched shrikes which flitted after the wildlife the water had disturbed. Later that morning the desert looked again as if nothing had happened.

On the way to Irikiri there wasn't even the shadow of a cloud in sight and when at last we reached the lake the sun was straight overhead and the car like an oven. The lake stretched as a shimmering pink line on the horizon: flamingoes indeed. In our eagerness to get close I drove straight at it, not realising that before a lake becomes hard desert it goes through a muddy stage camouflaged under a crusty layer which is not used to supporting cars. We went down to our axles in the vilest of malodourous substances. When we tried to move her out with the aid of a large number of tamarisk bushes we disturbed such a number of black stinging flies that we had to run for shelter. At last we got the car out again but had lost all energy to do anything but lie in the shadow under the car to wait for the sun to go down a bit. The flamingoes were out of reach but at least we could replace the question mark in our birdbook with one of exclamation.

We started to move again when it had become somewhat cooler and tried through plain desert to make for the track to Foum-Zguid which is at the head of a string of oases along a mountain. Our night drive became a delight. A pair of honey-badgers

flamingo

or ratels appeared in the middle of the track, looking like ordinary Irish badgers on which the black and white had become a bit mixed up. Following them slowly while they hobbled ahead and trying to make up our minds as to how we could pictorialise these unexpected apparitions, they suddenly dived into a burrow and were seen no more. Toads also appeared from nowhere, enormous ones of about a pound each. *Bufo viridis*, the green toad, is common all over North Africa; but we had not expected to encounter it so far into the desert; they are harmless beasts and have a fondness for houses, where they walk in to look for insects.

fenneks

Along the narrow clay paths through the oases fenneks — small sandy-coloured foxes with huge ears and great black eyes — were looking at us in the lights of the car. Delightful little animals often kept as pets by children, they live mainly on insects and other small animals and therefore frequent populated places where there is water and wildlife. In the open desert the most common rodents are the jerboas, also strictly nocturnal. Like tiny kangaroos they hop ahead in the headlamps at incredible speeds. They have large whiskered feet that prevent them sinking in the sand and long tails with a tuft for balancing. You never meet them in daytime for then they are hidden in deep burrows, protected from the heat, where also the humidity prevents too much water loss.

Through the south of Morocco runs a rather large river, the oued or wadi Dra. For most of its length it is seasonal and only near the sea is water in it all year. I am one of those people who gets restless if I have to go without seeing the sea for a couple of weeks and so we set off again, westward, back to a true river and the Atlantic. First we went down to Goulimine where a sign proudly proclaimed "Ici commence le Sahara" — a bit disappointing really for we thought we had been driving through it for weeks already.

Such places in the south were cashing in on the tourist trade, and enormous buses came straight from Germany and France. "Das rollende Hotel", a huge bus with a trailer containing bunks, was one of those enterprises: with air-conditioning, bar and toilets, it had it all. We met it, loaded with middle-aged German people, in a small oasis where it had backed into a palm tree and got stuck in an irrigation ditch. The whole village was out enjoying the diversion, the men shouting instructions and giving conflicting directions. At last a spot was found where the rolling hotel wasn't in anybody's way and everyone got out to savour the delights of an oasis. It was as if the circus had come to town and culture shock was experienced on either side. We had been in the oasis already for several days and so could take a detached view of the invasion which had in the meantime discovered that the oasis boasted a large pond, a holy well, in which holy fish — small barbels — swam. Too polite to point out to the tourists that one doesn't swim in holy water, and delighted to have a chance to see German ladies in bikinis, none of the men or boys objected until wives and mothers appeared to send the lot home and leave the visitors in peace. Mass tourism had come to the desert, and had started to destroy exactly what the visitors had come for.

Ten kilometres before we entered Goulimine we had picked up a hitch-hiker, the owner of a local restaurant by the name of "Perle du Sahara". His pearl turned out to be not much of a jewel so we declined his offer of eternal hospitality and sped on south to a place with the intriguing name of Tan Tan. Nobody could tell us what it meant but the small desert town turned out to be a tax-haven and the centre of an extensive smuggling business. There seemed to be plenty of money about and we received inflated offers for the landrover which we had to refuse. Our time was now more or less up and we had only a couple of days left to get to Casablanca where the coaster which was to take us to London hopefully was still loading tomatoes. After driving non-stop for a day and two nights we arrived to find the ship just finished loading; the car was hoisted aboard and within an hour we were on the Atlantic again, vowing to be back as soon as possible. Later that year on the television series we had a surfeit of camels, creepy-crawlies, sand and date-palms. I had entered a lasting love-affair with the Sahara and against all reason wanted to go back, and that was exactly what I did the following year.

Taking the boat from London to Casablanca, we had elaborate plans which began to founder as soon as we reached Tan-Tan again. The area was and still is hotly disputed between Morocco, Mauretania, Algeria and the locals who want independence, for many years now with guns and bombs. Tarfaya, south of Tan-Tan was officially a border post into Rio d'Oro — Spanish Sahara — but as Morocco claimed the region the local burgomaster would only give us a stamp in our passport that he had "seen us passing"

We had taken on Cascas, a local unemployed Touareg, as guide and companion and were lucky to have his company. He knew every sand dune and tent and taught us desert manners. Travelling in this region it is extremely bad form to drive past a tent. There may be someone sick who wants aspirins or even to be brought to hospital; maybe there are letters to be posted; they mightn't have seen people for weeks and anyhow, what's the hurry? So, according to the mood of the moment, you steer well away from tents or drive at them. Then the man will come out, throw stones at his dogs so they won't devour you, and after long and complicated greetings lead you into his mobile home, a seven metre wide tent of black goats' wool surrounded by a barrage of thorn bushes to keep the livestock out and the kids and lambs in. You are given strong mint tea and a meal; hospitality is generous and complete.

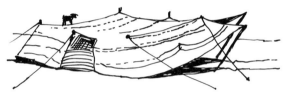

Etiquette requires that you drink three cups of the strong stuff. If you took only one, it would mean that there was maybe something wrong with it; so you have to accept a second and a third, but if you take more you're just plain greedy. We learned fast: never accept anything or eat with your left hand — this was based on sanitary considerations. You might ask after the health of the wife but you were not exactly encouraged to shake hands; in the Moroccan countryside women and girls still went about in public with their faces covered by yashmaks. In the desert the Berbers didn't bother, but one still would not approach a tent knowing that only the women were about; though with Cascas, who seemed to know everybody, we could be freer than if we had been on our own.

I was lucky with my companion for my second foray into the desert. David Shaw-Smith was not only a good cameraman but an inveterate snake and scorpion hunter and tireless collector of lizards — we ended up the trip with a desert zoo on top of the luggage. David also had a yen for archaeology. Wherever we stopped or camped we first inspected the ground for flints, prehistoric stone tools, scrapers, arrow-heads and other implements of which we found hundreds without really searching. We also found many small circular beads, cut out of the shells of ostrich-eggs, proof that this part of the Western Sahara had been formerly much richer in wildlife. One day drinking tea in yet another Berber tent our host produced an exquisite arrow-head out of his bournous and seeing the glint in David's eye immediately gave it as a present. Such are the manners of the men of the desert but if ever the political difficulties in this part of the world are solved and the country is thrown open to tourism this generous attitude towards foreigners is bound to disappear to be replaced with B&B notices and souvenir shops, phoney hotels in the shape of bedouin tents, bars and swimming pools.

In what is now Polisario country we had our first meeting with a sandstorm. In driving out of a wadi we had broken both the bolts that keep the back axle attached to the car. We had more or less fixed it with a rope but after days of mechanical protests and the loss of more bits and pieces than we could afford we couldn't go any further without doing irreparable damage. So, in the middle of the barest of dunes we unloaded the car completely; David stayed as watchman and Cascas and I drove gingerly south in search of El Aaiun, the capital of Spanish Sahara which was about 30 kilometres away, to find bolts and a welder. It was a memorable drive: in places the track had been swallowed up by advancing dunes and to find it again at the other side of the sands wasn't always easy.

At the border post which looked like a public toilet stuck in the middle of nowhere, Cascas couldn't come with me any further as he didn't have a passport — even though all his family were on the other side of the border. I soon entered El Aaiun where the car was quickly and efficiently fixed by a mechanic. Then after finding Cascas again at the border, we set off into the sandy desolation in the dead of night, its velvet sky and full moon.

It became a night to remember. We kept direction by the stars and the moon, not that I knew the names of the constellations but by keeping a particular bunch in the same corner of the windscreen I would know that I was more or less on the right course. Cascas had different ideas: he seemed to recognise where we were by studying the shape of the horizon, whereas to me, used to trees and grass, all dunes looked the same. After an eternity, and after I had counted at least four main complexes of sand dunes where on the way out we'd only gone through three, Cascas declared that we were lost. We clambered up a dune to sleep and there, at the other side, a candle was burning in front of a tent inside which David was snoring, the tent and all the luggage around covered in sand. There had been a local storm and he had fought a losing battle against the blowing sands. The next morning we dug everything out and loaded up the car which, with renewed vigour, brought us again to the border where we had to leave Cascas behind as we made for El Aaiun.

We had to present ourselves to the head of police, who didn't like us but couldn't find any legal pretext to kick us out. Did we have papers for Mauritania? No. Then they wouldn't let us in, unless we flew to Madrid to apply for visas or flew to Las Palmas, the Canary Islands, where the French consul might be able to give us the necessary stamps in our passports. In any case the chief wouldn't allow us to stay more than one night in El Aaiun; I don't know what they were trying to hide but there were thousands of Spanish soldiers about. We took the track to the airport where we hid the car behind a hangar and found a plane for Las Palmas. From the air the desert looked even more formidable than from the level of a car seat and we got some idea of what we had been travelling through.

The flight to Las Palmas was no more than a hop but the contrast could not have been greater. There was a bit of a beach, most of it having brought in by dumping Sahara sand. Everything else around appeared to be Swedish: even the Spanish dancers in a restaurant had come from Malmö. We had no success with either the French or American Consuls, and so we returned that night to Aaiun without any paper allowing us entry into Mauretania. We told the suspicous police chief some cock-and-bull story and left the capital of Spanish Sahara hastily, determined to get into Mauritania by hook or by crook.

We reached Mauritania but had to surrender our passports when we entered Bir Mogrein, Fort Trinquet of the defunct Foreign Legion. The local lieutenant was polite enough but he reasoned that if he wanted to travel in Europe he needed a visa, so we shouldn't be surprised that he was obliged to send us back. Why hadn't we gone to the embassy in Paris and got visas? Why indeed. We were allowed to camp outside the walls beside a long-dead donkey and some wrecked trucks, left-overs from the war. Sharing our feelings about Franco's police chiefs, he allowed us to leave the country to the north, into Algeria rather than via the westward track again, but not on our own.

We had to join a long caravan of greatly overloaded trucks on their way north. We seemed to be the only ones on the whole convoy who had had the foresight to bring a jack and a shovel, and every time one of the worn tyres of an overloaded truck punctured with great clouds of sand being blown about, we had to stop and render assistance. When we were safely out of sight of the army post we deserted the convoy and stormed ahead. With us we had a hitch-hiker, an Algerian merchant — in the desert one never refuses to take anybody — and later this man turned out to be sent by Allah, for he knew the people at the border and we were let into the People's Republic of Algeria without much trouble.

There was not much wildlife about. In one stretch of stony desert we had encountered a small flock of Houbara bustards, tall birds that run rather than fly, and filming those had been quite a sport. One of us would get out and set up the camera while the other would circle the extremely wary birds and try to drive them slowly into range of the waiting optics. The use of long tele-lenses in the desert has its limitations: the hot air rising from the soil blurrs all definition; the end result is very suggestive of heat but not much else. To get recognisable shots of birds you really must have them close which, in 25,000 square miles of desert, is a bit of a problem. Racing a fully loaded car over hamada — a flat plain composed of small pebbles — is great fun until, at great speed in the heat of the hunt and seeing nothing but the birds running in front of you, you overlook a small gully and hit the roof and the luggage in the back disintegrates. We managed in the end, at a price, to convey to Irish viewers what Houbaras looked like.

In Tindouf, the first town of importance we entered in Algeria, we had a serious encounter with the head of police who, after long arguments, allowed us to proceed. It wasn't so much that he didn't want us in the country: the problem was we had no official permission to use our cameras and there were a lot of military about. We came to a gentlemen's agreement: we were free to continue on our way if I promised not to take the camera out of the case. There was to be no Algerian footage.

I was tempted to strike straight north again from Tindouf back into Morocco, but the area was devoid of safe tracks into the Anti Atlas, the mountain chain at the other side. Morocco and Algeria had been at war and there were minefields about and probably soldiers. We decided to toe the official line and do the 802 kilometres to Béchar where there was a border post; into good old Morocco. 500 miles without a petrol station is a long way but we still had our hitch-hiking merchant who when the fuel-gauge was far into reserve during the middle of the night directed us to a military post where we got a fill-up again.

Béchar turned out to be full of enormous bars without any customers. The town had been the headquarters of the Foreign Legion but they weren't there any more to drink beer, and the other "plaisirs variés" had disappeared from the street. We felt as if we were in a ghost town or on the film set of *Beau Geste* after the actors had all gone home.

We arrived at a hamlet on the border at nightfall. I'll always remember the name of the little town as we were the guest of Boucif ben Boucif, chef de Police de Beni Ounif: it was an address in rhyme. Boucif had been a medical student in Paris when the war between France and Algeria started, had gone home, joined the army and when Algeria became independent had been rewarded with his job at the border. Used to the Parisian lights, he was bored stiff but saving up to get married. We got the whole story; it's amazing the things people tell you, a total stranger, when passing by like a ship in the night. Boucif, happy to have somebody to talk to, fed and feasted us for the rest of the night, and in the morning fetched the key to open the gate within the barbed wire fence that separated a People's Republic from a Kingdom. He warned us not to wander off the track if we didn't want to be blown up and waved us on our way.

Very soon we were stopped by a truck-load of Moroccan soldiers who told us that if we persevered on the track we had chosen out of some others at a junction, we would get into Algeria again and probably be blown up. Then they pointed the right way and we were soon in Figuig where oranges were half the price they had been in Algeria. We had a fruity party celebrating our safe return to Maghrib al Agsa. By now it was high summer and 42° in the shade but here ended our attempt to cross the largest desert in the world.

I may still do it one day. There are package tours leaving regularly for Oran and Algiers with barbecues on the way and cool drinks and soft beds in comfortable hotels. Personally I prefer to be woken up by a rising sun beside a smelly car, or by children in an oasis waiting in front of the tent to be entertained with "la machine".

Milka from Kap Dan, East Greenland.

the Land of Real People

FOR many years I had wanted to see the real Arctic and my chance came in 1969. The following year had been declared International Conservation Year and many organisations, committees, government departments and private individuals were climbing on the bandwagon. "Conservation of the Environment" was fashionable. The net result of all this turned out to involve more conversation than practical conservation but the Wildlife Service of the Department of Lands of the time announced its intention of acquiring, with the help of the World Wildlife Fund, part of the North Slob in County Wexford. Here, on either side of Wexford Harbour, between five and six thousand white-fronted geese of the Greenland race — about half the world-population — winter. The geese breed on the west coast of central Greenland and come down to Ireland in October to stay and feed on Irish grass.

If we could make their annual *séjour* in Ireland safe this would go a long way to ensure their survival. What could be more fitting than for me to go to Greenland and film the geese on their breeding sites? I prepared a budget, did some sums and tried to convince my friends in the department of the merits of such a film. My eagerness to go north was not tempered by cold Arctic reason, but the net result was that at the end of May 1969 my friend Micolo and I parked the old landrover under a "staff only" sign at Kastrup, Copenhagen's airport, and soon were winging our way over the Arctic Ocean in an SAS plane filled with real Greenlanders towards Sondre Stromfjord, the main airport of Kalagdlit Nunat, the land of the real people.

Our preparations had been quite thorough. We had done our homework and had in our pockets a number of letters of recommendation, permits and insurance policies. Our 98 kilos of excess luggage contained such items as an arctic tent, arctic sleeping bags, a rifle and an array of orange and blue lightweight items plus enough film stock to produce an epic.

The North Atlantic from a height of eight kilometres looked incredibly blue with here and there patches of floating pack-ice glistening in the sun. It was not hard to imagine them to be full of polar bears but as it turned out we did not see a single one during the whole summer we spent on Greenland. Not for the first time I felt that it is only from the air, travelling at 500 miles per hour that one gets an impression of how big the earth is.

The airport of Søndre Strømfjord is the social hub of Greenland. Anyone arriving has to pass through and if you wait long enough you can meet most of the 40,000 people who populate the largest island in the world. After a couple of days waiting, fogbound, we had the feeling that we knew and had talked to about a quarter of all Greenlanders. The immediate surroundings of the airport were full of wildlife and we wasted no time filming the caribou that swarmed around the airport, the great northern divers that bred in a lake behind and the family of arctic foxes which had their den under a heap of granite boulders on which an enterprising visitor had painted an enormous CND peace symbol. This was no empty gesture as the airport is part of the early warning system known as the DEW line and there is a large American garrison

and all kinds of mysterious and coldly dangerous-looking warplanes.

Arctic foxes are charming, fat and in some way cat-like with a silly little bark. Rather tame near the airport as nobody molests them, they live on what the hotel and the airforce provide in the way of kitchen refuse which also attracts large numbers of enormous ravens. Less dependent on mankind were the long-tailed duck that courted in a little ice-covered lake behind the airport and the large herds of caribou that crossed the swollen river where it runs into the fjord at the end of which the airport is built. Caribou are preposterous deer designed by a committee, not very intelligent but with sweet faces crowned by cumbersome structures like coat-racks constructed by an incompetent apprentice. They have widely-splayed hooves on which they literally dance over the tundra with a clicking sound emanating from their metatarsi. They were not very shy, far less so than our own native deer. We might be sitting in the tundra, scratching our mosquito-bites when all of a sudden a caribou would walk past; they always looked as if they were surprised at their own audacity. Arriving at the river they would at first hesitate and then, when the group became larger, the whole flock would cross like a swimming forest. It was spring, the river was in spate and the waters wild. Nothing would deter the animals. They often wandered over the airfield and when a plane was about to arrive a jeep, siren blaring, would chase them off.

The foxes provided hours of fun. The young especially didn't mind being watched; you could get them out of their dens by providing crumpled-up newspaper to play with. All over the airport there were posters warning one to take great care with foxes as they are carriers of rabies, which was rampant on Greenland. We heard some frightening stories of how airmen had been fighting off crazed and snapping foxes with towels while standing on wash-basins and other unsuitable refuges. So, we had to film our foxes with a rifle lying beside the camera, which made me feel an utterly graceless fool. Luckily our foxes were very healthy indeed.

It was a couple of days before we could leave the airport and continue towards the coast when at last the fog had lifted. From the helicopter that brought us to Jakobshavn we got a better impression of what we had let ourselves in for. In Ireland summer had started but here spring had hardly made its mark. We could see the awesome icecap: one long forbidding line of white; then the totally bare tundra with mosaics of small lakes still frozen over. We could see tracks where caribou had crossed the ice but that was the only visible indication of life. White, brown and black were the only colours under a sky of the purest blue. There are no words to describe the empty loneliness and the size of the place beyond the cosy confines of the airbase.

It cannot be said that Jakobshavn — Jacob's Harbour — the township from which we hoped to travel further, was a welcoming sight. Our huge Sikorsky helicopter landed on the tiniest and messiest of airfields ever, where we were soon surrounded by 98 kilos of assorted luggage and the local youth. At the airport there had been plenty of intelligible Danes, Americans and Greenlanders who spoke English but here hardly anybody did. Greenlandic is a language which bears no relation to any I know. Greenland's young people, however, are exuberantly welcoming and we were literally taken in hand and brought to Hotel Jakobshavn, run by an efficient Dane called Niss who spoke something we understood.

It is difficult to write about our first night in a Greenlandic township for how can there be night if it never gets dark? We were well inside the Arctic circle and wouldn't see the sun sink beneath the horizon for many weeks to come. We spent it sitting on the wooden terrace of Jakobshavn Hotel in a daze of disbelief at one of the greatest sights nature ever invented. Before us Disko Bay stretched out like a deep blue mirror with an army of incredibly enormous icebergs floating out on the tide, all completely soundlessly. A snowbunting with its nest under the steps sang on the balustrade, mosquitos buzzed and from time to time a shred of canine concert accentuated the air of utter peace. I had seen some big places but this was the biggest of them all.

Jakobshavn was a town of 2,700 people and double that number of sledgedogs. In summer there is no employment for these animals who are then half-starved and, because of rabies and their danger to children, are chained up in front of the small wooden houses and react with endless howling. An eskimo dog doesn't know how to bark properly but produces long-drawn wolf-like howls at the least provocation and in close disharmony with his colleagues. If 5,000 sledgedogs give a performance the effect is as loud as a Rolling Stones concert and slightly less tuneful to my untutored ears.

Jakobshavn is situated at the end of Jakobshavn Isfjord, which is fed straight from the icecap, 30 kilometres to the east, inland. The icecap covers 95% of Greenland and in the centre is about two miles thick; it is so heavy that it compresses the land underneath, which is not one large island but an archipelago similar to that of north-east Canada. Ice under pressure is plastic and flows slowly like water; it falls continuously off the sides of Greenland into the fjords it has gouged out over the millennia. Into the Jakobshavn Isfjord alone every twenty-four hours 25 million tons of ice descend, 100 by 100 by 100 metres every hour. The fjord is some 500 metres deep but at the exit there is a threshold at which the icebergs get stuck, at the same time relentlessly pushed from behind. Great tensions build up in the fjord, until at high tide the whole contents of it are more or less shot out into Disko Bay and hence down the Davis Strait into the Atlantic to melt on their way south.

We did not stay too long in hospitable Jakobshavn though we were still too early to go after the geese. We boarded a small vessel called *Tudglik*, the great northern diver, and headed north along the coast, the *Tudglik* being the official summer connection between the settlements along Disko Bay.

We chose to visit Sarqaq, a small settlement where people still made a living as hunters. The village is situated at the coast of Torsuqatak, another fjord that reaches from Disko Bay inland towards the icecap. The name Sarqaq means "sunny side of the mountain"; the settlement, which faces south with the snowy mountain range of Umanak Peninsula sheltering it from the north, is blessed with an exceptionally mild climate for Greenland. After a week on Greenland we had painlessly overcome our culture-shock. Greenlanders turned out to be the most hospitable and easy-going crowd in the world, full of laughs and devoid of inhibitions, and it had been very easy for us to make friends. We received solicited and unsolicited tuition in Greenlandic and soon became quite fluent in wishing everybody a good whatever-time-of-day. Greenlandic is the first language and Danish is the second; English comes a poor third as there is little contact with the Anglo-Saxon world.

The old burgomaster of Sarqaq, Hannibal Fencker, married to a charming Greenlandic lady, was the only resident Dane in the village apart from Paul, the schoolmaster. He had some English and was a mine of information. It was he, we discovered, who had provided most of the information we had gathered from the birdbooks we had scoured to learn more about the breeding habits of the geese. The news he gave us was not very encouraging. It had been a cold spring and there was hardly any grass in the valley a couple of days walk inland in Sarqaqdalen where the geese were supposed to breed. There would be a bad season. He gave us the use of a wooden building which had been left behind by Canadian mineral prospectors and we settled in as Greenland's newest immigrants.

In the line of wildlife Sarqaq was paradise: tame birds everywhere and a tundra flora that would burst into flower within weeks if the weather held. We saw some 5,000 brent geese pass by on their way to northern parts; phalaropes played at our feet in the harbour; we discovered the nest of a gyr falcon and nearby that of a peregrine. Arctic redpolls had a nest over the door and snowbuntings were as common as house-sparrows in an Irish village. Knots were courting behind the cemetery and a choice of wildfowl was passing at all times.

The time had not arrived yet to strike inland into the tundra but we made the best of our waiting time, filmed kajaks and people, went after beluga whales with Markus and Jens, two brothers we had soon befriended, and spent days digging in the

Beluga, kilagulak kakortak, hvidhval or white whale

thick banks of bones along the shore, remains of centuries of hunting where we found an assortment of flint scrapers and other implements the use of some of which had to be explained by the elders of the village. There was, for example, a tiny bone implement with a hole in it and a small eye at the side. One would never have guessed that it had been a valve sewn into an anorak through which air could be blown in case the wearer in his kajak felt cold or had to use his garment as a lifebelt. The small eye was to attach a sinew with a stopper at the end. There was another well-carved piece of bone that turned out to be a fastener for the straps on kamiker, women's boots of chewed sealskin. Some of the older people of the village still wore them and other traditional clothes but the younger ones were mainly in rubber boots and anoraks made in Copenhagen, and some girls were wearing the latest Danish fashions. There was a clash of influences and this became more than obvious the day the *Tugdlik* arrived once again to bring home some teenagers who had been to school in Denmark. Parents in traditional garb waited on the shore for daughters who stepped off the boat in fashionable clothes and high heels. The scene was embarrassing for both sides and it was clear that these youngsters would

never return for good to this forgotten part of the world after having tasted the city life of beautiful Copenhagen.

The quickest way to get acquainted with and be accepted in a tight community is, of course, to take an active part in anything that is going on. If I had been told in Ireland that within weeks I would be standing on an icefloe in a small eskimo harbour assisting in skinning a beautiful but dead beluga whale and gingerly chewing raw slices of its skin I would not have believed it. But such is life and I enjoyed it immensely however much my heart went out to the whale, especially when it turned out to have been expecting and the well-formed foetus, an exact replica of its mother, slid out, innocent and ivory white.

Belugas, in spring when they migrated along the coast up north to give birth, were the mainstay and food resource of the village. They are not difficult to hunt as they are rather tame and trusting. We went out several times with Mark and Jens to film the hunt and those of seals and killer whales.

The seals of Greenland's west coast are of different species than those we have in Ireland. There is the ringed seal, an animal resembling our own harbour seal and harp seals which I was to meet again in Canada.

Kajaks in Sarqaq, safe from the dogs

There is a considerable difference between the Greenlanders' hunting for the pot and the Canadians' doing the same on the grand scale for the skins of the pups and fishery protection: for the eskimos in the far flung settlements the seal is a main item in their diet, and the hunting is on a small scale. Even after many centuries of hunting whales and seals it is not the eskimo who is responsible for their decline. Canadians kill baby seals by the thousand for their skins and for a little of the shoulder meat; the rest of the carcass is left on the ice. Eskimos, however, use everything that can be eaten or made into something useful. The beluga whales are expertly and cleanly butchered and nothing goes to waste apart from the blubber, which is inedible and thrown back into the sea where it attracts great flocks of fulmar petrels. The white skin is a delicacy which tastes somewhat like fresh and greasy coconut and for which you need strong teeth. We learned to eat other unfamiliar things. Seal liver may be eaten raw and, as in the clean Arctic air things do not rot, a chunk of seal liver is taken on trips just as in Europe we would take sandwiches.

We spent a couple of weeks in Sarqaq, learned about the eskimo way of life and got to know practically everyone in the village, especially the children who all wanted to sleep in our tent which after a week looked as if it had been through a couple of wars. The dogs in the village roamed free and had to fend for themselves. It was one of the reasons why the kajaks, made out of sealskins stretched over a wooden frame, were kept high up on racks together with other comestibles such as dried fish. Meat was kept on a small island in the harbour buried in a deep snowdrift that wouldn't disappear before the end of summer and still provided meals from food caught the previous season. In Ireland one wouldn't dream of eating steak that had been out in the yard

for six months but in Greenland it doesn't matter much for the snow acts as a fridge and little rots away, even in high summer.

After weeks of this idyllic life we once again boarded the *Tudglik* when it passed by on its weekly round and went back to Jakobshavn which seemed to have taken on metropolitan allures during our absence. Man cannot judge size objectively but can only compare. For a couple of days we pitched tents at the edge of the icefjord in the midst of one of the most impressive landscapes I ever saw. In front of us the fjord was filled with gigantic icebergs, crunching and pressing against each other with some stretches of open water between in which ringed seal would appear and a choice of seabirds — tiny phalaropes, like us waiting for the tundra to thaw out, Brünnich's guillemots, the most plentiful auk in this part of the world, brent geese winging past in great flocks and long lines of King eiders low over the water. It was a magic spot.

At the corner of Disko Bay is a rocky head cut in two by a deep chasm. It was here we were told that in the past during times of famine old people who could no longer contribute to the economy of the tribe while still consuming food would voluntarily step to their deaths as a supreme sacrifice to the community.

Camp near Ilulisat

Micolo Delmonte and the author with Paul, the schoolteacher from Sarqaq, Markus Jensen and his son Anganguak. We visited the long and narrow fjord of Torsuqatak, on the west coast of Greenland, where over a million kittiwakes have their nests in one large colony, out of reach of all but rock climbers.

Jonas Jensen

Our neighbours were a family of which the father spent most of his time in town drinking instead of hunting the seal for which they had come. Greenland has more than its fair share of alcoholics. Anana, the mother, had to manage as well as she could. She used to point out guillemots which were swimming within rifle range. I don't like shooting birds, but now and then I had to oblige for, after all, we had to eat. The trouble is that when you shoot a guillemot on the water you have to get it on shore which in a fjord filled with enormous chunks of ice poses difficulties. Eventually the birds were fished out and Anana would pluck them deftly and boil them in their own juice which was later dished up as soup. Boiled guillemot tastes surprisingly good. We were also learning fast about which flowers were edible in the blossoming tundra and which ones to leave alone. When walking later through the hills and valleys we would be chewing continuously the showy flowers of the Arctic rhododendron or the lesser ones of the Labrador tea which the eskimos call *rajaksett* after the resemblance of the leaves to small kajaks.

Eskimos are splendid naturalists and know not only the names of all the plants, birds and animals they encounter but also what can be done with them. In Sarqaq we had been given a nicely illustrated set of primary schoolbooks by the Danish schoolteacher which made me conscious of how backward we are in Ireland in teaching natural history. The books became field guides for us: though the text in Greenlandic was unintelligible we learned all the names of the flowers and the birds.

The eskimos are very proud that they are the only ones who by sheer ingenuity and perseverance have managed to survive in a region which is under snow or ice some nine out of twelve months, where crops cannot be grown and where there are no trees. They don't like the word eskimo which means "eater of raw meat" and comes from the Cree Indian language and was picked up by the French when they colonised Canada. They wrote it down as esquimeau. Eskimos call themselves *Inuit* which simply means "the people".

a harp seal on pack-ice

With a glint in their eyes they will tell you how an ancient Inuit father discovered that his daughter was having an affair with one of his sledge dogs. That caused a scandal in the settlement and it was decided that dog and daughter were to be made *quivitok* — banished to a far island where they would have to fend for themselves. Quivitok used to be the supreme punishment for the most serious of crimes in the eskimo community which didn't know the death penalty. To be cast out of a group in the Arctic may, of course, be a punishment worse than death. Daughter and dog suffered that fate and after many years the father happened to come near the couple's island and somewhat remorsefully paid them a visit. He found his daughter and dog-in-law surrounded by children. Some of them looked quite human and others more like pups. He flew into a rage and killed all those that had tails and too much hair. And it is from the remaining half-breeds that all non-eskimos are descended. We are the non-Inuit.

The eskimo peoples have a long and complicated history marked by seven waves of new immigrants arriving originally from Siberia and later the North American continent. It is certain that there were eskimos in western Greenland as early as 600 BC. There are very few true-blooded Inuit left on Greenland; for many centuries their lines

mixed with the blood of Americans and Europeans — Dutch, Danes, English, Norwegians, Icelanders — and there are plenty of Greenlanders with blue eyes and freckles. But some of the original traits such as black and straight hair, absence of body hair and some less obvious traits remain dominant. The rich eskimo culture and traditions are dying out. Fibreglass boats and aluminium dinghies are taking over from indiginous native crafts; dog sledges are being replaced by skiddoos — motorbikes on skis — and discos are displacing traditional music.

In Jakobshavn too we made friends. There was Niss the hotel owner: he had

A female harp seal coming up through her bobbing hole in the pack-ice for a breath of air. Harp seals occur in the Arctic Ocean from Hudson Bay to Davis Strait and along the coasts of Greenland and Siberia. In much of their range they suffer from a senseless and cruel hunt when the pups, born on the ice, are killed by the thousand for their silky white fur.

The stack in front of the cliffs of Moher in County Clare is the home for masses of guillemots which lay their single eggs on narrow ledges without making nests.

come to Greenland for the same reason as most of the other Danes — easy money and no tax to pay for two years. He had grown to love the country, stayed on and was doing quite well. Tourism was about to come to the Arctic, most of the visitors being fed up with the Mediterranean and attracted by an ocean far bluer than that of the Côte d'Azur.

There are no roads out of town and the wilderness is only a kilometre away. There are taxis whose routes begin and end where the tundra starts and which are primarily used for the entertainment of teenagers chasing up and down the township. We attended a local dance called a *dansemik* where the people turn up in rubber boots and enormous anoraks with the names of popgroups painted on the backs. It reminded me strongly of a ceili I attended thirty years ago on Inishbofin, though on Greenland the relationship between males and females appeared a little less constrained.

Enormous supplies of prawns had been discovered in the deep of the Davis Strait and Disko Bay. At excessive cost the Danes imported a prawn processing factory, a triumph of modern technology, from America. However, they found that it was far from easy to get freedom-loving Greenlanders to take kindly to nine-to-five jobs in a factory, even a stainless steel one. So the factory was not able to attract enough people notwithstanding the high level of local unemployment and could not work to full capacity. This reflected too on the fifty-odd trawlers of Jakobshavn which were not allowed to bring in more than a token quota. The expensive factory had become a large Arctic white elephant.

Every small wooden house, scattered over the granite lumps of the town, had its own rack for drying fish in the front or back garden, the odd kajak also high up against being devoured by the ever-hungry dogs and implements and sledges all over the place. In most houses there were plenty of house plants, tomatoes fruiting in the porch and geraniums in front of the windows. In each house there was a large square iron tank containing chunks of melting ice for drinking water and children were perpetually fishing for these in the harbour to drag them home tied to a rope. The ice, originating from the largest glacier in the world bar Antarctica, makes the purest water.

When summer advanced the capelin spawned among the seaweed on the granite shore. They came in by the million, small salmon-like fish of some six or seven inches, running up the beaches where two males would take a female between them and fertilise the eggs when they were laid, the water becoming one churning milky mass of fish, eggs and sperm. Catching those wriggling multitudes was very easy and the whole town was at it. Standing in a boat one could scoop them up with a net and throw them straight into a fishbox and in an hour or so a whole boat could be filled. Others would throw them from the sea onto the rocks to let them dry, winter fodder for the dogs. The dogs themselves proved to be expert fishermen, wading into the shallows and having their fill. Children were foul-hooking them with a line and a treble hook at the end as a sport. It all made marvellous film.

Capelin, at the beginning of the season when they are not yet spent, are a lovely fish to eat fried in butter on a Primus stove. The eskimo name for capelin is *angmaggset* and later we were to travel to the east coast of the country to Angmaggsalik, the place where they spawn. Capelin are a very important fish in the ecology of the Arctic, not only for inshore fishery but also as food for cod, whales and seals. Unfortunately they are now fished on the grand scale by modern and efficient trawlers for processing as fishmeal, one of many examples of a squandering of resources.

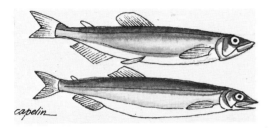

capelin

In summer a large passengership, the *Disko*, plies along the west coast of Greenland and visits all the townships. One day we went down with it to see other areas where we were told we could find our elusive geese. In Egedesminde — pronounced in the economical Danish tongue as "ayesminne" — we found the owner of a small boat who was going to Lersletten and was prepared to take us with him. Soon we were sailing through a vast archipelago of small islands inhabited by millions of Arctic terns and eiderduck. Gaily we sailed on, attacked from every island we passed by the most aggressive terns I have ever met and trying to avoid flocks of eiders reluctant to take to the wing. There were phalaropes galore and now and then a great northern diver would appear overhead, utter its mysterious call and show us the impossible way they fly with the head hanging down, differently from the way shown in ignorant bird books.

Within a day we ran into a thick fog and were soon totally lost. Our world had been reduced to a circle of fifty metres with only the screaming of the terns indicating that we were still near land. After a day we eventually found the channel that according to the map would bring us to an island that we had been told should be awash with geese.

When we arrived and walked into the wet and soggy tundra it turned out that the small lakes were still frozen over and there wasn't a blade of grass; it became clear that the geese had not arrived yet or were about to skip a season. Our trip was not in vain though: we met Arctic foxes, listened to the indecent calls of a multitude of ptarmigan and ran into a small herd of caribou who must have reached the island swimming. There also was a beautiful white gyr, the most impressive falcon of the Arctic compared to which a peregrine is but a little boy.

We returned again to Sarqaq and were received as old friends. Eskimos must be the most filmed people in the world. As their civilisation is about to disappear completely, drowned in modern technology, industrial greed and to a lesser extent in alcohol and all the other blessings of modern civilisation, quite a few film crews descend each year into eskimo villages to record for posterity the decline and fall of an ancient and independent people, who of course resent the intrusion into their privacy and dislike being treated as monkeys in a zoo. So I was especially glad that we were welcomed again and given all the help we needed.

Markus Jensen brought us out to the beach around the headland, some distance along the coast from where we hoped to walk through Sarqaqdalen, a wide and beautiful valley, to its head where whitefronts were possibly breeding at the lakes. The weather was fine when we disembarked on the sandy beach through a few million capelin whilst a pure white Arctic fox was watching the new arrivals in his valley. At last the quest for the elusive geese had begun in earnest. We were rather heavily laden with food for more than a week, cameras, tent and gear, a rifle and sound equipment. There were flowers everywhere, showy Arctic poppies, rhododen-

Making friends with rock hyraxes, Ein Gedi, Israel.   Merlin van Gelderen

A Moroccan green toad (Bufo viridis)

drons, Arctic azaleas -a choice of heathers, a riot of lichens of all sizes, textures and colours. The tundra in flower would be a cheerful place if it were not for the mosquitoes also enjoying the fine weather. During the following days we often wished for rain, wind or snow to keep them down.

Tundra stretches out over permafrost, the permanently frozen subsoil which causes water not to drain away but to stay in pools, puddles and marshes which make the going very slow. There were also innumerable shallow rivers to cross. To prevent our toes falling off in the glacier waters we had brought diving booties, but putting these on and off all the time became cumbersome so we sloshed on in rubber boots full of water which warmed up nicely after a while. It proved to be quite impossible to expose even the smallest bit of skin to the elements as we were travelling in the centre of a constant cloud of the most ferocious insects I've ever met anywhere. When we cooked our porridge for breakfast the steam attracted even thicker hordes than the sweat of our brows. We started off by picking them out of our breakfast but soon gave that up as they didn't make that much difference to the taste and added some proteins and probably badly needed vita-

mins to our diet. We had brought some tins of insect repellent with the suggestive name of "OFF" which worked as long as we kept it liberally dripping off our faces; when we became sunburnt and scratched, however, it hurt even more than the stings of the mosquitoes. To follow even a call of nature became a painful problem which we were never able to solve.

I had read Fritjof Nansen's *The First Crossing of Greenland* in which he describes how he and his companions after incredible hardship managed, on skis and dragging a boat behind them, to cross the icecap from east to west. He tells about the worst day of this incredible journey when at last they were in the western tundra again and describes how bare hands covered by the insects came to look like mittens and how it affected their mental health. In Sarqaqdalen I began to understand what Nansen had been on about and also why nobody in the village had shown any willingness to come with us.

the harbour of Sarqaq

88

There were compensations on our journey: the fox that walked up with us part of the way, the birds and the flowers and now and then the remains of past eskimo activities — ingenious stone traps for foxes, a dam across the river formerly used in fishing for char. There was a singing Lapland bunting every hundred yards of the way, there were knots and other waders, inquisitive snow buntings flying with us, and the call of the ptarmigans. Knowing that we were the only people in the whole of the long, wide valley caused a special exhiliration which is hard to explain.

We had agreed with Markus that he would pick us up again at the beach at a certain date and we knew that if we didn't turn up he would radio for a helicopter to search for us. After all, we had been obliged by the Danish authorities to take out expensive insurance against just such a happening, but apart from some stupid accident not much could really happen to us.

In Ireland if one is so inclined one can believe in leprechauns, in ghosts and little people, in things that go bump in the night, shadows of ancient evil that might make you pitch your tent backed against rocks or under a tree. But here, on our trip into the interior, I never got the feeling that something or somebody was watching us or that it was desirable to put a bit of bread as an offering on the hungry grass. There was a feeling of total innocence in the landscape.

We made very slow progress through the soppy tundra. There is a system in such circumstances that makes you go on, at least it worked for me. Struggling with that idiotic pack on my back, my boots filling up with water for the umpteenth time, mosquitoes in my eyes, rumblings in my stomach and cramp in my legs, I would decide to have a rest but not just yet — a few hundred yards further on a clean and comfortable granite boulder positively blinked at me and then I would take a break. And when I reached the boulder I would discover that I was not half as exhausted as I feared. So on to the next lump of granite. There I would fall down to be immediately attacked by even thicker droves of tormenting insects and realise that horizontally I was more attractive to them than in the vertical and in that case I might as well walk So, driven on by mosquitoes, we at last reached the head of the valley.

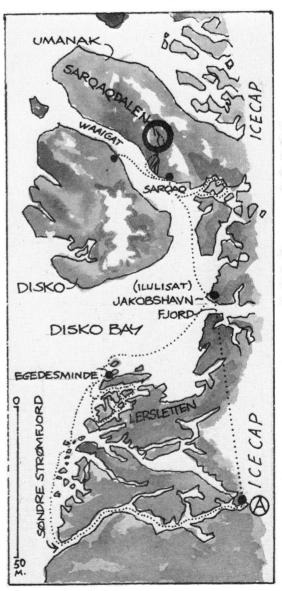

89

Dragonfly, Everglades, Florida.

Cascas, our companion in the Sahara, breaking a loaf of sugar for the tea.

Dorcas gazelle beside an acacia bush in the desert.

At different stages along the route we shed expendable parts of our luggage and our progress was marked by a series of cairns: the tent, film cans, clothing, a hefty tape-recorder, the rifle, pots and pans — all things you can do without if it comes to the crunch, all to be picked up on the way back. The tent hadn't really been necessary: the weather was balmy and we slept snugly, covered up against the mosquitoes in our bags in dry bits of tundra. It was the height of summer and there was no difference between night or day, the sun circling the heavens on a near horizontal course.

A striking aspect of the Greenland tundra was the absolute peace and quiet. When walking there was the rub of your trousers, the clinking of a spoon in a pot in a rucksack, the squash of the water in your boots, but when at last you were sitting down on a boulder the silence would in a physical sense fall around you and become painful in your ears, the loudest noises the beating of your own heart and the clear little song of a far-away Lapland bunting.

Lapland bunting

We had walked for days when we at last met the first geese, a couple of families with small goslings who had seen us long before we saw them. Some more geese went by in the far distance, in pairs, with no sign of young. A single bird standing at the edge of a lake two kilometres away looked promising but it flew up long before we got anywhere near and a combing out of the whole area revealed no more. It was, as Hannibal had feared, a poor season and the bulk of the geese were probably somewhere else or didn't breed that year. We had

against us the fact that in the flat tundra there is no way that a human can hide. In the high vegetation the geese have no trouble concealing themselves and all the odds are against the intruder. We had been led to believe that whitefronts bred in colonies along the lakes but it turned out that they were spread out very thinly on the slopes of the mountains and only frequented the lakes for courting, returning with the goslings and later for moulting.

As our time in the valley was up we returned to the coast, the way we had come, collecting our belongings as we went. At the coast we had a day to spare before Markus would come to pick us up again. Here the river spread out in a wide delta between innumerable islands on which knots bred and little stints and other birds we only knew as migrants in Ireland. We felt that our trip had not been in vain, even though the only shots we had of the geese and their offspring were rather distant ones.

Between the islands there were shallow bits that had been nicely warmed up by a summer of Arctic sun and we decided it was time for a bath as we were to return to civilisation. So, slowly peeling off layers of clothing and gradually descending into the lukewarm Arctic waters we at last gave the mosquitoes a chance to reach a few of the parts they hadn't had a chance to reach before. We were still scratching when Markus arrived in his aluminium dinghy to bring us back to the village.

In Sarqaq we were lucky enough to scrounge a lift from a visiting dignitary who turned out to be Greenland's prime minister himself, an ardent angler who combined pleasure with duties and brought us back to Jakobshavn on his boat, visiting settlements and prime fishing spots on the way; this gave us the opportunity to see some more of the settlements along Disko Bay. Visiting friends is a popular pastime on Greenland, in summer by boat, in winter by sledge or skiddoo; Greenlanders always seem to be on the move, and about everybody agreed that travelling in winter was more fun than in summer. As far as mosquitoes were concerned we could well believe it.

Back in Søndre Strømfjord we tried in vain to get permission from the military to travel to the legendary Thule, a settlement on the extreme north-east point of Greenland where eskimos still lived untouched by civilisation until the whole village was moved on by the American military who needed a base. It was understandable that they didn't want us there. However, another plane was leaving for the east coast, to Kap Dan and we were on it, crossing the ice cap again. In the middle there was another DEW station where huge Hercules airplanes landed straight onto the ice and mysterious buildings vaguely reminiscent of oversized white Byzantine churches were supposed to keep the so-called free world safe. It looked vaguely menacing.

Kap Dan, its airport hidden between snow-covered mountains, was bleak and forbidding. All non-Greenlanders seemed to be either American or Danish military and airport staff. There was a hotel where we settled and watched newsreels flown over from Washington and old television programmes, together with the airmen and their local girl friends who were allowed to stay week-ends. Food was good and plentiful and parties were in progress at all times.

The village itself, Kulusuk, was far more primitive than Jakobshavn and the terrain and climate less wholesome than on the balmy west coast. Loftleider had just inaugurated regular day-trips for tourists from Iceland, weather permitting. The experience was a remarkable one from either side: a party of mixed tourists, some of them dressed to kill, stumbling over the rough track from the airport to the village from which the children had gone out to welcome them, not knowing what to expect and then the meeting with the locals in their Sunday best, beautiful seal coats and trousers and embroidered jackets, the babies and children all done up for the occasion. Milka was there, a venerable old lady and probably the only one who in those days was still wearing the traditional topknot. She and her grandson gave a demonstration of Greenlandic singing accompanied by a drum, a strange and melancholy sound. The tune itself, though, was easy on the ear and you could hum along with it. Milka had widely travelled with a folklore group and was a lady of the world.

a kajak, a boat made to measure

In Ireland and other European countries we eat only a few of the fish and shellfish in which the sea abunds. In poorer countries people are less choosy. Here, Sri Lankan children are fishing with a cloth for planktonic copepods — tiny crustaceans — in a lagoon along the coast. The grey mass is made into a delicious curry.

The Greenlanders were just as anxious to know the tourists as the other way round. Kulusuk had been in great isolation up to the days when the airport had been established. European influence was far less than on the west coast. Here were still a fair number of kajaks, somewhat different in design from those out west, and Eno, a very old man, gave a demonstration of how to right the elegant craft in case you capsized, turning over and over again until his eyes were streaming and he was sniffing like a seal. The tourists' visit to the village could only be a short one. After clambering back along the flowery track, accompanied by the youth of the village, with much waving the whole party boarded the plane again to return to Iceland, delighted to have met for once "real eskimos"; no doubt the villagers also discussed the strange ways and dress of their temporary guests. We stayed behind and felt rather as if we belonged to the local community.

Years later, with a party of Irish people with whom I had been travelling Iceland, I returned to the village. Milka was still there singing her song but in the meantime the children had learned that you could sell trinkets for real money and that every lady in the company would be good for sweets. It was good, though, to meet old friends again and we ended up having a great Irish-eskimo party in the wooden community hall where the men sang bawdy songs for Irish redheads, all the Greenlanders roaring with laughter. We ended up singing Irish ballads which greatly impressed the village and only at the very last moment, when the fog was closing in, got back to the airplane, arm in arm with the locals.

From Kap Dan we took the ferry to Angmaggsalik which turned out to be a township without much smell or taste and attended yet another dansemik by way of social diversion, but our trip was about over and nearly all our film was shot. We went back to Søndre Strømfjord and from there returned to Copenhagen where ye olde landrover was still standing under the "staff only" sign without even a parking ticket. We were home within a week.

the village of Kulusuk, East Greenland

'Progress' has reached Greenland. Empty fuel drums and a small boy in the harbour of Kap Dan.

When all the film was processed and printed it turned out that we had enough for an interesting series on life in the Arctic with plenty of wildlife — seals, birds, flowers, whales and broad eskimos smiles even though as a study of the life of the Greenland white-fronted goose we had failed. I hope that one day I'll be able to go in search of the geese again. I'll camp then with as many cans of mosquito spray as film tins at the head of Sarqaqdalen for a whole summer, ignoring the sight of icebergs and all other Arctic delights.

IN 1975 I set off to drive overland to India, with Daibhi Doran, who also worked in the film business. We intended to stay away for three months, ended up staying four, and we drove 17,500 miles.

It would take another book to relate all the adventures we had, first crossing through France and Italy into Yugoslavia, then on through Bulgaria to Turkey, crossing the Bosphorus, on via the main road to Teheran and then through Afghanistan and Pakistan into India itself. It was a trip I will long remember, not only because of the deserts and mountains we crossed and all the new and strange animals, birds and flowers we met, but above all because of the people we encountered.

"Sir," said the impeccable customs official in Atari, where one enters India from Pakistan; "Sir, this carnet is invalid." We filled out endless forms stating what we had with us in the form of valuables, but soon enough we sailed into the Indian Punjab and were on the road to Amritsar and the Golden Temple of the Sikhs.

If I were blindfolded, bundled into a plane and dropped anywhere I had been before I could make a fair guess, by my nose alone, as to where I had landed. Morocco smells of heat and hash, Greenland of dogshit, and India would be the easiest to recognise. No other country on earth gives so much olfactory stimulation. The smell is not a sick one or dirty but a mixture of dust and earth and sweat, mouldering ruins with an indication of fungi, a unique and very earthy blend. In towns and villages there is the addition of fruit and flowers, spicy food and no mean hint of religion, whiffs of incense. In India one is never far from a village: there are 900,000 of them, so the *mélange* of perfumes is always there, changing with the seasons. When the monsoons drop their rains and the country bursts into flower the accent is on vegetative wet.

After beautiful Amritsar the road to Delhi was wide and crowded with oxcarts, camels, bullocks, cows, people and bicycles, and it was bordered with mango trees on which the fruit was not yet ripe. Growing on the branches which they use as support were great clusters of flowering orchids. We had arrived at the height of the hot season and the landscape was scorched, apart from where, along canals and river banks, huge and thick reeds hid a multitude of birds that were quite new to us. There were pied kingfishers and white-breasted ones which we call Smyrna kingfishers in Europe. There was our own little kingfisher and another one with an enormous beak, making it look completely topheavy. There was a choice of bee-eaters: dainty little green ones, blue-tailed and brown-headed ones, all very easy to distinguish by their English names for the early colonisers hadn't shown much imagination in naming birds new to them. A bird looking like something between a crow and a pheasant is called a pheasant crow; a bird that behaves like a robin but is patterned like a magpie is a magpie robin; and identifying white-spotted fantail flycatchers or white-breasted kingfishers presented no problems.

pied kingfisher

We passed a small village on our first day and explored a ruined and deserted temple covered in luxuriant climbers and noisy monkeys; children came out and offered us slices of melon. All around there were bits of statues, broken and discarded gods and a colony of rose-ringed parakeets had their nests in the hollows. An Indian roller bred in a hole in the wall, exploding into a bright-blue apparition when it came out. That first day in India was a revelation. In view of a number of tanks with rather fierce-looking soldiers on the road we found a track away from the main road and camped along the Sadluj, one of the rivers that give the Punjab its name, which simply means "five rivers".

We had arrived in India at the wrong time, at the end of the dry season. In the dry and dusty land there wasn't a flower in sight apart from the jubilant flame-trees that

bonnet macaque

Sleeping on top of the van I woke in the morning at an ungodly hour to see in the rays of the rising sun over the river an unmistakeable deer the size of a small dog dance away over the track. It was a muntjac or barking deer which proved its point by giving a fair imitation of a tired terrier when it saw that the bus was alive after all, before disappearing in the rushes. A pair of mongooses entered upon the unworldly scene, rolling along as if on wheels and looking neither left nor right, passing underneath the van without even giving it a glance. Twelve feet away a paddybird stepped along the track, mynahs and red-vented bulbuls added their voices to the morning chorus which surprisingly contained a few ordinary blackbirds. On the river a line of cormorants passed by for a morning's fishing. A line of villagers armed with hoes passed by. If they were surprised to see us standing there in the middle of the track they didn't show it but greeted us earnestly and profusely and then walked on, not even looking back.

decorated towns and villages like trees on fire. Later, driving into Rajastan, the heat became quite unbearable. It was hotter than I had ever experienced in the Sahara.

Delhi is enormous and pleasant. We had some official business and we changed money from pounds into rupees. In view of our restricted budget and not knowing how long we would spend in the country, we lived as economically as possible, camping when we could, cooking for ourselves and becoming experts in getting the maximum amount of heat out of a minimum number of sticks and branches. Life in India was cheap indeed, and shopping was fun. In a market you would point at a heap of onions or fruit and as most people don't have much English in the country you'd show a rupee for which you would then get a few kilos and a large clay pot thrown in. At the next stall you would discover garlic and for another rupee another pot was filled. Along the roads there were tea stalls, huts of branches and cow-dung, where for one quarter of a rupee you'd get a glass of sweet tea with milk. In many of these places you would be given the tea in a small clay cup which you could throw away after use. The stalls were surrounded by layers of broken cups which crunched underfoot.

All kinds of experts had given us dire warnings and advice about the precautions we would have to take so as not to end up with a number of diseases affecting body and mind: only drink bottled water, boil anything you eat or drink for at least twenty minutes. Tea should be comparatively safe, so we had been told. Never bathe in open water, never eat unpeeled fruit, etc., etc. We had a book about tropical diseases which would scare anybody off going anywhere more southerly than the Costa Brava.

The Coca Cola available in the villages was made with the same water as the tea, and while boiled tea might be safe, what about the bowl the cups were washed in? Of course, we took reasonable care and didn't drink out of puddles or rivers and didn't swim in stagnant water: the book was too explicit about the joys of bilharzia — a dreadful affliction caused by a liver parasite which uses a freshwater snail as host — nor did we walk around in bare feet through which hookworm might infest our innards. We did take our weekly pills against malaria and for the rest trusted on healthy constitutions and the assorted collection of antibodies we were sure to have collected during the weeks we had been on the roads of Asia.

We had some accidents. The worst of these was when a hammer had an unpleasant collision with my nose, breaking it and provoking vast gushes of blood. I thought I was going to bleed death where I lay under the van but I surprised myself by taking it calmly and considering cremation on the banks of the Ganges or maybe a burial beside a particularly nice pond in the jungle where we had stayed a while. There had

been a forest of lotus flowers and jacanas, long-toed waterhens designed by Salvador Dali, and a troop of black-faced langurs, the most elegant of all monkeys whom we had filmed picking lotus leaves and folding them neatly before chewing. I had had visions of a teak garden seat with an inscription in my honour. But the bleeding stopped after what seemed hours and before two weeks passed the little loose bits of bone under my facial skin had knitted together. It took another month before I looked normal again.

After Delhi we descended southward to find the Keoladeo Ghana sanctuary near Bharatpur, the most spectacular waterbird sanctuary anywhere: a vast spread of shallow water and fields, wet even in the dry season, with countless ibises, egrets and storks of many species. Most of the migratory birds had left for the sub-arctic and the locals were waiting on nest building until the wet season. Still, there was enough left to keep the cameras whirring.

Never had I seen so many waterfowl together: darters, painted storks, marabout storks, just storks, ibises, cormorants and a whole row of different egrets with long-legged red- or yellow-wattled lapwings and a score of duck; tall sarus cranes and a choice of small waders, not to speak of masses of turtles, snakes, butterflies and lizards. Here we had our first meeting with the strangest of Indian antelopes, the Nilgai (blue cow) which were big and ungainly, a sort of horse-like deer full of horns and tassles in odd places. They were a joy to watch munching the babul-trees, the local acacia, and we filmed them from our cool room in the guesthouse. Other big game was about too: herds of wild boar of the Indian variety, thin, mean and lean with a crest of black hair on the back, looking like perman-

indian wild boar

ently angry dogs. Waterbuffalo were there in plenty, herded by little boys — illegally.

Wherever one goes in India, one has company. It is hard to get used to being surrounded at all times by a circle of polite spectators, silent and friendly. It is even impossible to go for a leak on your own. When we were sitting in the shadow of a babul tree on one of the narrow dykes through the reserve, we would soon be surrounded by all the small boys from within a circle of a mile at least who would watch our every movement and discuss among themselves what we were doing. Older boys, speaking English, would strike up a conversation which nearly always ended on the same note — what about a job for them in Ireland?

We had a pleasant meeting with a delightful bird, a white-spotted fantail flycatcher, much smaller and more elegant than its name. A pair was building a nest in a thornbush and let us observe proceedings from a couple of feet away. To film them wasn't easy as they were in the shadow but with a small pocket-mirror we projected the sun into their abode which didn't bother them in the least and made a nice sequence. India turned out to be full of flycatchers, all tame and trusting. Of the paradise flycatcher our birdbook said: "The agile fairy-like movements of the male as he twists and turns after flies in the air, with his tail-ribbons looping or trailing behind, is a spectacle of exquisite charm." I couldn't have described it better myself.

One day, when camping along a stream we were watched by a solemn great horned owl who also didn't mind being photographed. In a village we found an assembly of at least thirty vultures earnestly pulling at the abhorrent remains of a long-dead donkey, adding yet another dimension to the perfumes of the east. The birds hardly stepped aside when I trod amongst them for some close-ups. India is strong in biological refuse-control. In villages roaming pigs devour anything organic, scruffy dogs eat unmentionables and vultures go for big dead things. There is little in the way of plastic about and the system works quite well. Each village has a dheel, a pond which serves, among other things, to water the buffaloes which every evening descend with their attendant small boys into the muddy water, not a very hygienic sight but utterly picturesque, with paddybirds, small brown egrets, flitting to and fro to peck up any insect-life disturbed in the general hubbub.

Anybody we had talked to before we departed had assured us that India was populated by one vast mass of starving people, all holding out their hands to be fed or for money, making travelling the countryside one long assault on one's guilty, well-fed western conscience. It wasn't like that. The picture painted by the western media is only partly true; we certainly met with poverty on a scale unknown in even the most destitute parts of Europe; we were in large cities where multitudes lived on the sidewalks with hardly any shelter; we met with lepers, beggars and cripples; we certainly had to adjust some of our notions and values. But on the whole, during the months as we crossed the subcontinent, we found the Indians a healthy and cheerful lot. Maybe we didn't look too deeply into the caste system; we weren't robbed by dakoits; we didn't enquire into social wrongs though we were certainly not blind to them. It was not, however, in the brief which we had given ourselves, which was to film some of the wildlife and the natural wonders of this exciting country.

In Kanha, one of the many huge National Parks, we could not ignore how this tiger reserve had been set up, partly by money supplied by the World Wildlife Fund, partly by money from Delhi. Tigers live on deer and deer live on grass and shrub. It is an easy sum to work out how many acres of grassland one needs to feed one tiger. The grazing has to be exclusively for deer, no domestic livestock is allowed in, so, in order to create a reserve, the families of the sub-sistence farmers of the area had to move out. They had been given new wattle and mud houses outside the reserve. We could not judge if the compensation had been fair. It certainly did not appear so to the uproot-ed families who periodically set fire to the sal and teakwood forests and poached in what was now state property.

In Kanha reserve itself, which when we arrived boasted forty-four tigers where there had been only twenty or so before, a few families were left, working as foresters, trackers and mahouts — elephant drivers. We were staying in a nice little bungalow on a hill with elephants behind the house and a choice of wildlife passing by at all times: jungle cats, jackals and a lot of smaller animals such as palm squirrels, mongoose, in a delightful setting in a forest of high sal trees. We paid very little for our bungalow, some 75p per day but we must have been very rich in the eyes of the shy and raggedy children who were collecting sal nuts in the forest. It was very hard to make friends with them — they ran when they saw us. Eventu-ally we worked out that they made about 10p a day by selling the nuts to some firm in the nearby town. Their parents, workers in the estate, were hospitable enough and invited us for drinks at night, fearfully strong stuff made out of fermented cashew nuts.

We had meant to stay for only a weekend in Kanha but the desire to see a real live tiger kept us from leaving. Each morning, an hour before sunrise, we would mount one of the elephants and set off into the bamboo jungle, and each morning the mahout would assure us that this day was going to be *the* day. Though we never came face to face with the "fearful symmetry" my memories of these early mornings are among the best of the whole trip. As we glided high through the bamboos, behind the mahout, on top of an elephant whose innards softly rumbled,

pushing to the side stems that might hit one in the face, all around an incredibly varied morning chorus of birds, it did not really matter that once again the only traces of a tiger were footprints in the sand along a track or river. At least we learned to distin-guish between the feet of male and female tigers, the first fitting into a square the latter into a rectangle; both fearfully large. The trackers knew each individual tiger by its footprints.

Tigers are large but terribly secretive; we were told you could pass one by hidden in the tall grass or reeds six feet away and you wouldn't see it. Like many animals, tigers have a safety distance. Stay outside that circle and no tiger will attack and as the king of the jungle would see you long before you noticed him, it was highly unlikely that you would ever get close enough. No one in the reserve seemed to have any fear of the animals; they were much more afraid of the leopards, which were more unpredictable. One morning we watched one watching us from the top of a heap of giant boulders waiting for the sun to rise; at least we had seen one kind of big cat.

An animal we were earnestly warned about was the sloth bear, an untidy digger into termite heaps which would suck the insects up through a gap between its front teeth. For that occupation the beast needs neither good hearing nor good senses of smell and sight. You could come upon one around the corner of a track in the jungle and as he had not seen you coming he would have had no time to retreat: you would be well within his flight distance and would be attacked immediately, with dire results. Years later, in the jungles of Sri Lanka, I got the same warning — never get close to see what a sloth bear is doing — but there at least nobody was afraid of leopards of which the Sri Lankan forest people are rather fond.

जिन्दगी से बढ़कर
कुछ नहीं.
NOTHING IS MORE
PRECIOUS THAN LIFE.
म.प्र. निर्माण विभाग (भ./स.) पन्ना

a reminder on the road to Kanha

sloth bear

The manager of Kanha, a young bachelor who was an ardent photographer and spent three-quarters of his £45 monthly salary on film, became a dear friend and because of that we were afforded certain privileges denied to day-trippers. Officially one was not allowed to be in the park after dark or tread the jungle on foot — both, of course, rules with good reason.

There were several species of deer, the most common being the chital, spotted deer or axis, a superbly elegant and charming animal, three feet at the shoulder so of about the same size as our sikas. You would meet them in daytime resting in the forest and see them moving at dusk. In the dark, you would meet a herd travelling along a forest track and if you switched off the light they would pass the van without any apparent fear and you could touch their backs through the window. Sambar, another species of deer, far bigger than the spotted ones, could also be met at night, and the third deer, the barasingha, a very handsome animal, could be seen in the open during daytime. Deer-spotting presented no difficulty and filming was easy.

A special thrill was to see gaurs, the Indian bisons, enormous animals that combined all the best in bovines. The bull's shoulder height is often well over six feet when they may weigh as much as 2,000 lb. Luckily they are shy and peaceful. During the day they retire to the shelter and seclusion of the forest and come out at night to drink. When we were waiting for them to appear in the dusk we would first see white socks in the shadows and then, with some hesitation, a small herd would come out into the open, a breath-taking sight which unfortunately was very hard to film, though on one occasion we succeeded.

Mr Dubey, the manager, took us one day to a tiny village way off the beaten track where a religious festival was being organised. Part of the village had been made into a temple, full of exhuberantly painted statues made from dried cow-dung. All the gods and heroes of the Indian pantheon were there: Krishna playing his flute while sitting in a tree, Ganesha with his elephant's head on a human body, son of Shiva and Parvati and bringer of good fortune. There was a bright red Hanuman, the monkey god, King Ashok, giants and dwarfs, and musicians, warriors and sages, all fashioned out of (to us) the most unlikely of art material. Cow-dung in India has many uses, dried as a floor covering, as fuel and here as a modelling medium. The figures were not the handiwork of the villagers; they had been made by specialists in a neighbouring hamlet and had been paid for with the equivalent of £160, an enormous sum. The outdoor temple was not to be a permanent affair: during the coming monsoon rains first the colours and then the figures themselves were bound to be washed away.

white breasted kingfisher

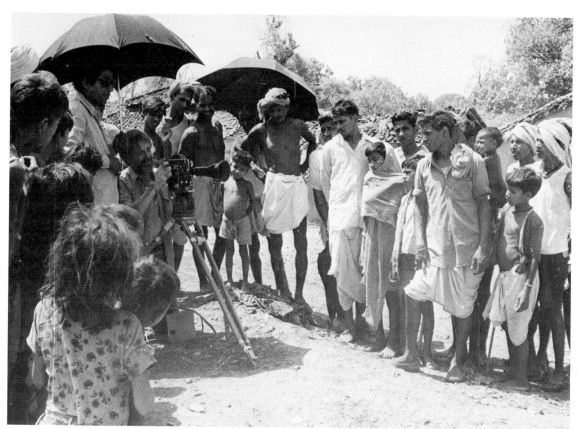

filming in an Indian village   *Daibhi Doran*

The villagers told us that we were the very first foreigners ever to visit them and graciously gave us permission to film their garden of the gods and so, surrounded by a pushing crowd, on bare feet as is the custom on holy ground, and with Dubey holding his black umbrella over my head, I filmed the most touching temple we were ever likely to meet.

In a bigger place nearby we did our shopping. This was an earnest and rather complicated business. When we stepped into the grocery, all our new-found friends entered with us to give advice and encouragement. Asking for rice, we would be given ten samples. I never knew there were so many different types. After some deliberation I pointed at a particularly nice looking lot and asked for a kilo of it whereupon the crowd expressed amazement at my expertise. In a society where money is very scarce the spending of it is a serious and time-consuming business. When we had our victuals, the shopkeeper would write out the bill, spend ten minutes arriving at a total and ask us to check his totting which would then be inspected again by some bright teenager.

In this haphazard account of our wanderings through India it is easy enough to jump from Bharatpur, which is not far from Delhi, straight over to Kanha, the tiger reserve in Madhya Pradesh, but there were an awful lot of miles between the two, especially as we drove a rather erratic course. From Delhi we wandered down into Rajasthan, skirted the Great Rann of Kutch, the hottest desert I had ever been in, and stayed a couple of days in Bombay, a fascinating and terrifying city with about four times as many inhabitants as the whole of Ireland. From there we went south first to have a dip in the Indian Ocean and from the coast we crossed the heart of India with the intention of ending up in Varanasi before calling it a day and turning west again.

On the way we had visited some of the country's most famous tourist attractions. The Taj Mahal in Agra had been just too perfect for words. Its splendour is certainly not overrated but to me it appeared too sterile, too polished, too devoid of life. We had not been let in with our cameras as we had no special permission from the Department of Antiquities, so by way of revenge we used long lenses and filmed from the outside. It looked just as well. Jaipur is a city in Rajasthan, famous for the Hawa Mahal, the Castle of the Winds, an incredible eighteenth century building with a front of red stucco lace of perforated windows which we filmed from all sides without an official in sight, surrounded and cheered on by half of Jaipur's inhabitants. Rajasthan means literally "abode of the prince" and is the traditional homeland of the Rajputs, a proud tribe of conquerors. Nowhere else in India did we see such a collection of mighty palaces, diverse landscapes and cheerfully painted houses. We could have driven for years through the state and still have gained no complete picture of its incredible richness and diversity.

That observation applies also to the whole of India which is much more than a homogenous country composed of a number of states. To me it became a new world, so vast and varied and of such unfathomable complexity in its history, religions and cultures, that — though we were armed with plenty of guide-books and had done our homework in advance — I must confess that after a month of driving through forests and jungles, plains and mountains and visiting temples and ruins, I was more confused than I had been on entering the country at Amritsar when at least I nurtured some preconceived ideas.

It was safe to stick to wildlife; there no confusion was possible: it was easier to distinguish between a rhesus macaque and a common langur than between a Jain and a Hindu temple, more difficult to decide if we were standing in front of an inscription in Sanskrit or in Hindi than under either a teak or a sal tree.

In Khajeraho there is a vast complex of temples dating from the tenth to the thirteenth century, a site so enormous, so unbelievable and unforgettable that it is irrelevant that I am unable to remember the names of the ancient kings who built these hollow mountains from which thousands upon thousands of stone gods in all their manifestations — warriors, kings, dancing girls and the whole of the Kama Sutra — looked down upon us in our little Volkswagen van. There is one name I do remember from Khajeraho: "The Eternal Arts Emporium", a tiny shop where for little money I bought a reputedly thousand-year-old bronze toy elephant on wheels and where the proprietor gave us the address of his brother, a taxi-driver in Varanasi who would "see us right" in the way of food and accommodation if we ever ended up there.

We had more recommendations. In an eating place (Masala Dosa 1 rupee 25 paise) we had made the acquaintance of a flowery yogi in the company of a covey of admiring girls. He suggested we visit a friend of his, a hermit-priest who lived in an old temple not far away in the middle of the jungle. We had seen enough temple ruins to last us a lifetime but we were interested by the news that the place was beside a pool at the foot of a waterfall. The weather was extremely hot and we had seen no water other than mucky village dheels for days. We could do with a dip, so, armed with a letter from our friend which we couldn't read apart from the sacred "oum" symbol on top, we set off into the wilds.

We couldn't find the place at first but we met two students in a village who had been there before and they brought us to a gorge where we parked the car and descended towards a beckoning pool. The temple was there too, a tumble of stones, and so was the hermit, a rather hairy and unsavoury type. The whole scene was as idyllic as could be with the trickle of a dying waterfall, the luxurious jungle all around us, birds singing, butterflies fluttering from flower to flower, toads and frogs galore calling and croaking against a solid wall of variegated greens with only the ruin reminding us that we were in India and not in primeval paradise. Even so, I felt there was something vaguely wrong with the place.

We collected wood and made a fire and soon a pot with mixed vegetables was bubbling away. All of a sudden, out of nowhere a swarm of wild bees descended upon us. Before I had time to jump into the lake I was stung all over the head; the others fled into the dark recesses of the temple where our hairy hermit was muttering away, quite uninterested.

The situation was ridiculous. If out of the jungle a tiger had appeared we would not have been half as scared as we were of that dark buzzing cloud around our pot and the fire. No way was I going to brave it to save the soup. After a long time watching from the dark as our meal was being overcooked, one of the students, deserving a medal, grabbed a bucket and doused the bees, pot and embers. Slowly the buzzing subsided and we could sneak away from the place, still hungry.

In the van again, speeding away, the students told us how, on the very spot we had parked, only a week earlier a band of dakoits — highway robbers — had waylaid a bus, relieved all the passengers of their possessions and set the vehicle on fire. It had been the hermit who had sheltered the dakoits. The yogi's letter was then produced and translated: a recommendation to take good care of us. It wasn't too clear in what way that was meant, but we took no chances and fled as fast as we could to the relative safety of the highway.

Few tourists travelled the country as we did, and it was obvious that most of the villages and towns were not used to westerners. Sometimes producing a camera caused no end of excitement and often we felt in need of crowd control, even in a city like Delhi which isn't exactly a provincial hamlet. There was an old man, deftly making, out of lengths of aluminium wire, intriguingly complicated and charming toy bicycles. It was a welcome activity to film, for in nature-films variety is the spice of wildlife. In no time we were surrounded by a circle of onlookers. This was the late Mrs Ghandi's Delhi and there was a prohibition in force against public gatherings. With the old man muttering that he would probably be arrested as the cause of the commotion, we had to film fast, before the police arrived. The toy bike we bought for 24p and we hung it as a mascot from the mirror in the van. Wherever we went later all the children we met wanted to see and have it but I was firm and have it since at home on the mantelpiece, a small memento of Indian ingenuity.

pheasant-tailed jacana

This capacity of making something nice out of the simplest of materials, something of beauty or practical value out of waste I found one of the charms of India and the Indians. Nothing broken is thrown away if it can be repaired: empty tins are made into kitchen utensils, old exercise books into bags for groceries, discarded light-bulbs into ingenious oil-lamps, any type of sheet metal recycled, any scrap of paper or plastic re-used, and worn car-tyres made into sandals.

On the whole Indians live vegetarian lives. In the USA the meat consumption of the average citizen is 110 kilograms per year, in India just over 1 kilogram. In western India in the state of Rajasthan the desert is encroaching and drought is becoming a permanent phenomenon. Forests are felled at a frightening rate, threatening watersheds and further impoverishing the already exhausted land that has to feed a fast-growing population. An average Irish city dweller uses some 175 litres of domestic water, an Indian villager less than 40 litres from wells, and less than half the Indian population have access to safe drinking water. The availability of clean water, of course, is the single most important factor in fighting disease. Trachoma, scabies and leprosy are spread by insufficient water for personal hygiene; typhoid, cholera, dysentery and diarrhoea are helped along by contaminated drinking water and defective sanitation is a mighty aid in starting epidemics.

Indians are, compared to us west-Europeans, extremely proper. There are separate male and female cinema queues; topless bathing on public beaches is out; but nowhere else have I seen so many people uninhibitedly defecating along the road. The abundance of scavenging dogs, vultures and free-roaming pigs is certainly a help to sanitation, though I wouldn't ask for a pork chop in a restaurant if it were on the menu.

I vividly recall my first meeting with a leprosy sufferer. Passing through a village we saw a queue of women at a water tap. I joined them in order to replenish our supply, under the misconception that water from a tap is safer than if it comes straight from the ground. The woman in front of me turned to allow me to go first; even at a water tap you are an honoured guest. She could not speak: where there should have been a nose and a mouth there were only gaping holes. It was then that I started to ask myself what the hell I was doing there, filming pretty birds and landscape.

In Bombay, at the waterfront near the famous Gate of India, in the splendid Taj Mahal hotel we consumed ice-cream at the comparatively outrageous price of five rupees, and very nice it was. Around the corner on the pavement whole families were living without water or sanitation. I have always felt that it would be a very good thing if Europeans, even if only once in their lives, could see how the other half lives, and could realise also that "the other half" is more likely three-quarters of all the people on this earth.

We learned that there are several ways to approach India and we met practitioners of all of them. There were the wealthy tourists who came to see the Red Castle in Delhi, the Taj Mahal and all the other splendours; they stayed in stylish, expensive hotels never seeing any of the thousands of small villages in which the greater part of all Indians live. There was another, very large contingent of Europeans, mainly young, who were living a life of squalor in Indian cities, attracted by cheap drugs and the low cost of living. There were the starry-eyed youngsters who came after encountering Buddhism or Hinduism in Europe but soon discovered that not all Indians were living according to the Bhagavad Gita or could quote Rabindranath Tagore, the great poet, and that the more you see of Hinduism the more complicated, contradictory and unfathomable it becomes. It is one thing to chant Hare Krishna on the streets of Dublin or London, it is another to do the same on the banks of the Ganges.

In Varanasi we wrestled the car through the crowded, narrow streets filled with pilgrims, cows and rickshaws, to find the taxi-driver brother of the Eternal Arts Emporium we'd met in Khajeraho. Instead of asking for him at his stand at the impressive, European-style Varanasi Hotel, we yielded to the temptation of comfort without hassle and for once booked a room. For the next couple of days we explored the holy city, a large number of its thousand temples, saw the cremation of the dead on the ghats — the steps that lead down to the river — and joined the pilgrims who had come from all over to be purified in its coffee-coloured waters. To them, the Ganges is God himself.

One morning, in the cool of the dawn, we descended the ghats; the river looked as if it were filled with olive oil. Bhurs — enormous, rickety wooden sailing ships — passed by, snail-like and silent, the helmsmen standing on raised platforms on the afterdecks. A light fog was swirling over the mirrored surface. The opposite bank, about a mile away, a dirty yellow beach, wide as if the Ganges were an ocean, not a river. Pilgrims were chanting and performing their morning puja, sitting or standing in the water and letting it run through their cupped hands. On a ghat nearby a corpse in a white cloth was washed in the river; later it would be burned. Flowers, colourful little boats, were launched onto the holy water.

Sadhus and Nirbanis, holy men, stark naked but smeared with ashes and cowdung sat in huts, tinkling little bells. At a food stall one came up to me and asked me to buy him a meal. Choosing a pound of boiled rice and one onion, he refused anything more. Polite conversations with other men sitting under parasols, nothing philosophical, just small talk. A bright-red thumb-mark on your forehead when leaving: a blessing. A wrinkled old woman, apparently asleep on a bed along the street, only after passing by did I realise that she was dead. And then we found a boatman to row us out onto the river and a couple of charming little boys to come with us as guides.

spotless cows, decorated with beads, at a market

tottering temple ruins in a jungle

The Ganges first sees the light of day in the Himalayas where it emerges from an ice-cave at a height of nearly 14,000 feet. In this cave Ganga, daughter of a nymph and a king, was persuaded to come down to earth to redeem from hell the souls of the 60,000 sons of a King called Sagara by purifying their ashes. Ganga was assisted at her birth by Shiva, through whose hair she was allowed to flow to earth. This is one version of the story; there are many more.

From the mountains to the Indian Ocean south of Calcutta the river is 1,500 miles long; and for the millions of Hindus it is the most venerated river on earth. To drink the water of Mother Ganges and to bathe in it is to wash away guilt. To be cremated on her banks or to have died there is the wish of every Hindu. The Shannon is the Shannon' is the Shannon but the Ganges has no less than 108 names and the translations of some mean "whose water is a mine of nectar", "dwelling in the water-pot of Shiva", "carrying away fear", "creating happiness", "holy and perfect", "full of fish", "dwelling in Shiva's head", "eternally pure", "eternal", "destroyer of sin", "a light amidst the darkness of ignorance", "roaming about rose-apple-tree island" — and that island is India. Quite a river.

Negotiations about the price of taking a picture of the three largest elephants on the road to Varanasi: asked three, offer one, settle for two cigarettes each.

Daibhi Doran

fishing in a lotus pond

Varanasi has a thousand temples, we had been told, and we could well believe it as we looked at the city from the river: a mountain slide of buildings descending to the bank. From the water the individual chants of prayer mingled, with here and there a rusty-sounding loudspeaker to increase the volume, accentuated by the rhythm of splashing oars, a hazy musical backdrop to a quite unearthly scene. After a while we unconsciously joined the chanting, and it was days before we got the tune out of our heads.

All of a sudden there was a loud splash as a dolphin surfaced for a breath of air and fell back into the water. These strange fresh-water dolphins are blind and find their prey by echo-location. We tried hard to take pictures of the animals; they were plentiful enough but it was impossible to forecast where the next one would be surfacing. We saw white-winged terns and cormorants too, obvious signs that there were plenty of fish in the river. A score of vultures floated past on the carcass of a hapless water buffalo. During the morning it became un-comfortably hot again and, trusting in the purifying properties of Ganges water and the anti-cholera injections, with my mouth tightly shut, I had a dip, feeling a great deal better afterwards, if not holier.

Varanasi more than any other city endeared Mother India to me. It seemed a world unto itself at the centre of the Hindu universe. It was unique, different from Rome or Lourdes or the holy city of Anuradhapura in Sri Lanka. On the one hand it disgusted me and on the other hand it was the most charming and persuasive of all Indian cities. We were stepped on by cows, ripped off by some people, given presents by others and invited into houses; we joined a wedding procession, had endless discussions with sadhus, and were swallowed up by the life of the city.

Nobody who has a soul can leave India without having been touched where it counts, in the heart. Some because of the richness, some because of the poverty and others because of the wisdom; but for whatever reason nobody goes home unchanged.

In a Sri Lankan fishing village

an unspoilt island?

I DON'T want to give the impression that I spent the years between the sixties and the present solely coasting carefree through deserts and having tea with tribesmen; most filming was and still is done in Ireland. Over the years I visited every county and I got to know many places but it was inevitable that I developed favourites.

There are some places for which I have not been able to feel much enthusiasm. I have never been overfond of Connemara; it depresses me. There are either endless bogs or tiny little fields giving me claustrophobia and when it rains, which is too often, I have to flee. Admittedly, the sight of the Maam Turks on the horizon causes some excitement; but it is of a different order to what I experience approaching the landing on Saltee or coming down the Conor Pass into Dingle.

I am still on a voyage of discovery and can't claim to know every corner of Ireland yet. If asked to name my most favourite spots I would be hard pressed for an answer but the Burren in County Clare would certainly be among the first three. I had thought that over the years I had been on every green road, had explored every turlough and valley, but only the other day I found a new boreen that must have been there since the beginning of time or at least since people first tramped the grey mountains. Each time I go back I find something new: an orchid that had previously been elusive, a pothole I hadn't fallen in before, lizards, a new peregrine eyrie, or some other delight in this most un-Irish of Irish landscapes.

Nowhere else have I found the same ringing rock, the same clarity of light over limestone. I did discover a similarity in the Karst of Yugoslavia where the rock and the dry-stone walls are the same, but when you look over them you find tobacco rather than grass and mountain avens and ancient sweet chestnut trees instead of whitethorn. Above all, the Atlantic is missing. Another landscape that reminds me vaguely of the Burren is the island of Öland off the east coast of Sweden where there are even more wild orchids than on Ireland's limestone. There are no hills and the sea is brackish and shallow and only offers a few thousand eiderduck by way of compensation.

The Burren has over the years become a prime tourist attraction. In the old days when Lies and I used to camp on the dunes of Fanore, the only ones in the area, we drove through a hard-to-find gate and then had the whole of the place to ourselves, camping on top of a dune facing the Atlantic, with the single red light of Aranmore winking at us. At the time we were not the only tourists; there were Germans and French botany professors with their students, who stayed at Keane's Hotel in Lisdoon. They were searching for orchids and studying the remarkable flora, an amalgam of Lusitanian, Mediterranean and sub-arctic elements: Alpine spring-gentians blooming side by side with Mediterranean orchids and mountain avens, a plant that should have stayed on the tops of high Scottish mountains, or in Iceland, Spitzbergen or Greenland.

Maryangela Keane, a botanist, did more than anyone else to make the area popular, writing a splendid guide to the flowers, giving lectures and hosting international botanical groups in her hotel. British pot-holers also discovered the Burren. They explored and mapped the cave-systems along the side of Slieve Elva. A cave discovered by the late Jacko McGann in 1944 was opened to the public in 1973. Now the Aillwee Cave — with a splendid reception building truly in harmony with its surroundings, built from local stone and only made visible from afar by the buses and cars parked in front — is a tourist attraction of the first order.

The proliferation of hotels and eating places inspires mixed feelings. Apparently unhindered by regulations the area is now covered in a brutal collection of advertising signs and hoardings, each one trying to outdo the competition in bad design and clashing colour. So far only the main roads have been disfigured and there are still plenty of uncontaminated boreens left.

Only the most drastic of measures might restore the once pristine face of the dune-complex which has over the years been covered by an assortment of caravans of all ages and in all states of delapidation. But there are still plenty of pyramidal orchids and centaury to be seen in the dunes, and even bee-orchids. The marten-cat still combs the beach of Fanore and a mile or so away at Black Head you may surprise an otter or two, a privilege that has become rare elsewhere in Europe. In the Burren the pine-marten, arguably the rarest animal in Ireland, has one of its strongholds.

Years ago, John MacNamara of Fanore, who in his own way is an expert on the animals, found a den with young and on a glorious June evening we set off in the hope of films and photographs. It became a night to remember. Leaving the road at the big boulder at Ballyryan we walked the limestone cliff and sat and waited opposite Dúnan Mór. Out of the haze came the noisiest badger ever which started to dig, puffing and grunting. A fox walked past, hardly looking at us and from below, at the foot of the cliff, came the sound of young pine-martens at play, screeching among the boulders.

Seeing something without reaching for a camera makes me feel guilty, as if I am getting something without paying for it. That is the result of twenty years of seeing the world through a viewfinder. I usually feel better if I can think up a good excuse: either it is too dark, or it has just started to rain, or I am out of film. In this case the excuse was even better — a camera would have spoiled everything, the purr of the camera's motor would have been an intrusion.

I had seen pine-martens occasionally crossing the road and once one galloping from grike to grike over a Burren pavement until it saw me and dived for cover. I had never been really close. Now my microphone was hanging down the cliff — at least I was getting some sort of souvenir. As I hoisted it up again it got stuck, I peeped over the edge and there was a marten-cat looking at the mike and then at me, two hairy faces with four feet between them. It was the closest encounter ever and I am still hoping that it will happen again when I am looking through a viewfinder in good light.

I have some other favourite places in the Burren. One of them is a small depression not far from the coast road. There is an enormous badger-sett with entrances and exits all over the place and usually a fox as a lodger in one of them. A good-looking ringfort sternly stands nearby and there is a low wall for cover. If the badgers are not out yet and the fox has gone hunting there are always rabbits to look at and no few hares either while a wheatear is collecting daddy longlegs for its young and burnet moths are traipsing over sweet thyme.

Another fine place, not far from Mullagh More, the most peculiar of Burren hills, lies after a bend in the green road where you meet a hidden farm and as an added surprise a marsh in the narrow valley with a bit of a lake left in the centre. It's covered in the frilly flowers of bogbean, and usually a solitary and very white goose to offset all those subtle pinks and greens amid the grey of the rock and the cream of the whitethorn. Then the walled track meanders on again uphill.

Not long after arriving in Ireland I made a friend, who was as much a fan of the Burren as I was to become. Dick Deegan was a self-made photographer who had his studio in Leeson Street, Dublin, and travelled on the proceeds. At one stage of his eventful life he had set himself the task to photograph every wild orchid that could be found in Ireland, a daunting prospect which I guess was only a pretext for being among the grey hills of his favourite county. Over the years I got to know him rather well as he travelled with me on several occasions, once to explore the wastes of Iceland and on a trip to Tunisia where he not only charmed the other members of the tour but the natives as well.

Dick Deegan on Iceland

Kairouan in the centre of Tunisia is a holy city with a beautiful and venerable old mosque, one of the very few in the Arab world where non-muslim visitors are welcome, after some formalities. These entailed signing a paper that you would behave well and be decently dressed, not unreasonable considering the scant respect many tourists show for religions and traditions not their own. Dick though wouldn't have any of it. He always declared to be a traveller and not a tourist. I still am proud he classed me in the first category. He put on his little Tunisian red felt cap and with his false teeth in his pocket because of sore gums, mumbled Salem Aleikum, two of the three words in Arabic he knew and walked into the mosque, unchallenged and mightily pleased with himself. Later during the trip he got lost in Tozeur at the edge of the Sahara and was eventually found back seated in the centre of a large audience: all the children and half the shopkeepers of the town to whom he was telling stories, drinking their tea and eating their fruit, mishmish, apricots.

Dick's photographs were brilliant and unlike any others taken on that memorable tour of Tunisia. No wonder, they were traveller's pictures and not tourist's snapshots. He was also an excellent teacher who gave many a budding snapshooter a boost which often took the form of a gentle kick in the pants. He met his maker in South Africa. Having applied to join an expedition crossing Africa by landrover from north to south, for which the age limit had been set at 35, well over 60, by sheer personality, he had been taken on. No doubt he had become the life and soul of the party. His last picture postcard said: we are now leaving the plains and entering the rain forest — and we had been looking forward to his stories and pictures. He died in Johannesburg of a heart attack and I believe this may have been the way he wanted it — to go out as a traveller and not fading away in a Dublin hospital. I don't know if he ever finished his self-imposed project of picturing all the orchids in the country. His slides were made into a short film after his death but it didn't really work — a sharp Wicklow voice was missing.

fern symmetry

The hills and valleys of the Burren have kept their character and wild flora not because they were left alone by mankind but because of the system of land-use over the centuries. If people had not kept livestock and farmed much more of the landscape would have been covered in dense hazel scrub and there would have been far less open ground. It is still a debating point among experts as to whether there ever have been great forests in the Burren. Be that as it may, husbandry is partly responsible for the wealth of wild flowers, among them a number of rare and special species. The carboniferous limestone in all its different formations absorbs heat in summer which is slowly released in winter; the rock acts as a giant storage heater. That, combined with plentiful rainfall and good drainage, makes for naturally good grazing where cattle can be left out in the field all year long. The damage to the wild habitat is done when landowners start to apply fertiliser in quantity. That may improve the yield but wild flowers disappear, especially those that have very specific requirements such as orchids, the most sensitive plants of all to changing conditions.

A dandelion may produce seeds which sprout the following year producing flowering plants again the same season. Orchids aren't that easy-going. Their tiny seeds first have to find a fungus in the soil and a specific one at that. The fungus invades the seed, which partly feeds on it and so the microscopic seedling is able to do for a while without green leaves, which only come at a later stage. Later the baby orchid is able to survive without the fungus, but that takes time. In some species it can take ten or more years before at last there is a new flowering plant. That makes orchids very special and explains why they should never be picked.

In most European countries orchids are totally protected but in Ireland we haven't got that far yet. In any case, protection by

cock stonechat

law of wildlife is no more than a token gesture. For many years now most Irish birds and animals have been protected by law, but if ever anyone is brought to court for the illegal killing of protected birds — it rarely happens — the fines are ridiculously small. From time to time spectacular rare birds turn up and ospreys, buzzards, egrets and not long ago an American belted kingfisher have been shot by misguided sportsmen. If a pigeon-fancier who sees a peregrine falcon take his birds shoots the falcon, I can't condone but I can at least understand. Why somebody would have a potshot at a cattle-egret or a kingfisher is beyond me.

Every time I am in the Burren I see people digging up plants to take home for the garden. Orchids are not transplantable, they'll die for sure. Sometimes specialists are the worst offenders. The Burren is the

ant on catsfoot

annual playground for learned botanists from many countries, stern professors with great herbariums in their universities, and it can be dangerous to point out anything rare to one of them. You turn round and there is nothing left but a hole where *Neotinea intacta* once stood. It has happened. Another favourite is *Ajuga pyramidalis*, a weedy thing, I believe, which I have never

been able to find between the caravans on the Fanore dunes. To a real botanist it is worth its weight in gold. The tourists who carry off geraniums (bloody cranesbill) by the armfull do less damage. They grow like wildfire and are neither easily missed nor eradicated. As for taking hazel branches for water-divining the visitor has every farmer's blessing.

'I say, my good man, where do I find this Burren?'

To protect its riches, the Burren should be made into a large National Park; it would rank among the best in Europe. Farming and grazing would not cease; on the contrary, life would go on very much as it did before. There would, however, be a controlling body, composed not of hacks, politicians and fanatics but by responsible, level-headed specialists, to see that no harm is done to the landscape or special habitats. Commercial developments should be controlled, perhaps more through education than by having a big stick behind the door.

So far local bodies have not been able or willing to prevent eyesores such as the forest of advertising hoardings on the main roads, brutal housing developments in beauty spots, senseless "land-improvement" which only profits single individuals, and so-called services to the tourists which will eventually drive away the very visitors on whom many in the Burren depend for their livelihood. The Burren is special and if we keep it that way it will be to everybody's advantage in the long run, not only to bird-watchers and botanists. It is heartening that the people who live in this blessed corner of County Clare are, on the whole, well aware of the beauty around them and the special status of the area.

The slobs in County Wexford, at either side of Wexford harbour, house an enormous number of wildfowl and waders in autumn and winter and I have filmed there over and over again from the very beginning of the programmes on RTE. The slobs are mainly famous, and internationally so, for the large numbers of Greenland white-fronted geese that winter there, as many as about half the world's population.

It was not always so. The geese need grazing on a variety of grasses for survival and for building up of fat-reserves to be used as fuel for the long trek back to their breeding grounds in mid-west Greenland; they need a supply of fresh water and a safe place to spend the nights. In the past there used to be far more of these places in Ireland than there are now — lake islands, bogs, fens and moors or coastal marshes. More and more of these areas have been "developed", drained and exploited and there seems to be no end to the spoilation of the traditional habitats of the geese. That many of the areas are of internationally recognised scientific importance, and are even officially protected, doesn't seem to matter. However, geese are adaptable: if yet another of their haunts is made uninhabitable, they move to new sites.

The Wexford slobs have over the years become something of a large refugee camp, and as is the case with many such places it has become permanent. The North Slob was reclaimed from the sea in the middle of the last century in the Dutch manner: it was dyked in and the land was drained through a pumping station. The original one is still there, its now smokeless stack the highest point over the flat polder. The fields are large, separated by ditches, and farmed. Wide channels into which the ditches drain, meander down to the sea-dyke and in the mouth of the Slaney river itself there were sandbanks and islands on which the geese spent the nights, safe from disturbance and predators, an ideal situation which was discovered by more and more geese as the years passed. At the beginning of the century they started moving in and by the thirties there were already thousands of whitefronts. Precise counts of the birds came later and now all through the season their numbers are carefully monitored.

In the early sixties the North Slob was bought by go-ahead and efficient farming interests who, with grants from the Government, started to drain the lands further. One of our first programmes about the slobs opened with a shot of an enormous heap of drainage pipes and an expression of fear concerning the fate of the geese. Luckily "soup is never eaten as hot as it is served" and some of the fears of impending disaster were never realised. Rigid controls on shooting were introduced; part of the North Slob was made into a wildfowl reserve, from which not only the geese benefitted but countless other birds as well; a public viewing tower was built and a visitor's centre; in a way the geese had "made it" and the situation is quite healthy at least for the present. The geese also proved to be more adaptable than everyone thought. Notwithstanding the fact that their traditional roosting place, Tern Island, had been washed away during a number of gales, they found different banks in the harbour. Also, a lot of agricultural produce, spilled wheat in the stubble and young grain, provided nourishment, to be made into goose-fat during the winter and spring.

It is no wonder that a yearly expedition to the waters and the wilds of the North and South Slob has become a sort of tradition. We get romantic shots of the whitefronts rising or falling in, and pick out geese of different species among the multitude — pink-feets, a couple of barnacles or a Persil-white snow-goose. But we also go for the Bewick's swans, the vast numbers of waders and, above all, the landscape that, more than any other in Ireland, reminds me of the Dutch polders where I did my early bird watching.

It is hard to get close to the geese; they are watchful and wary making it difficult to get them in close-up pulling grass and hissing with outstretched necks at members of neighbouring families. The birds, especially when the season advances, are used to tractors and cars going up and down along the pot-holed farm road and so if you stay in the car you get as close as two hundred yards from them. Oscar Merne, who for many years was warden on the reserve and did daily counts from a white Volkswagen beetle, could get closer, for the geese had got used to his insistent vehicle. Geese may have bird-brains but are far from stupid and one has to be content with long lenses.

Of all the venues in Ireland which have provided fodder for my lens in the line of birds, none has been as prolific as Bull Island in Dublin Bay. I more or less started my career there with endless shots of oystercatchers digging for worms. I have become hesitant about aiming my camera at them any more; if there still are people in Ireland who don't know what oystercatchers are — the big fat black-and-white ones with the long red beaks — it certainly isn't my fault.

Another favourite Bull Island bird is the brent goose for which I have a very soft spot. No larger than mallards, they come all the way from Arctic Canada, even further away than Greenland, to graze on seaweed and grass between the rubbish, the plastic bags and old car-tyres in Dublin Bay. They are birds for which you don't need a hide of any sort, which you can watch comfortably without binoculars or long lenses while the traffic on the Jim Larkin Road rattles past behind you; birds that will feed on the golf-course, hardly moving for club-toting civil servants.

oystercatchers!

a tight flock of dunlin on Bull Island in Dublin Bay

There's more than oystercatchers and brent on the Bull, of course. There are masses of waders in season, thousands of wildfowl feeding on the saltmarsh and parading on the water when the tide is in; shoveler, wigeon, teal, mallard and shelduck and, to keep the interest of twitchers going, the more than occasional rarity. The Bull has bred more bird watchers per acre than any other bird-spot in Ireland. When the annual avocet, blue-winged teal or other ornithological delicacy arrives, phones start ringing and in no time at all the whole bird-watching fraternity reports sick from school or work and can be found on the causeway and along the mudflats.

Dubliners don't know how lucky they are. There are few capital cities in the world where one can do one's birdwatching from a double-decker bus as one can on the coast road near Bull Island. Indeed, Irish people in general don't know their luck.

a blue-winged teal from the U.S.A.

It would have been nice if I could have ended this book on a cheerful note, if I could have looked back over the thirty years and chronicled the achievements of the authorities and of our legislators in protecting and enhancing our island environment. It would have been nice to have been able to report on:

- the joys of bathing safely in a clean Dublin Bay;
- the strict planning controls that prevent monstrosities being built in beauty spots;
- the lively interest taken by politicians in environmental matters;
- the complete disappearance of rubbish along our roads;
- the chain of national parks and nature reserves effectively protecting all of our precious national heritage;
- the splendid Viking museum at Wood Quay;
- the unselfish love for hares expressed at open coursing meetings;
- the pristine state of our rivers and lakes;
- the utmost care with which every farmer disposes of pig slurry and silage effluent;

- the assured future of the Atlantic salmon as an Irish species following the ending of all illegal netting and over-fishing;
- the general regard for and effective application of the Wildlife Act;
- the safeguarding of internationally famous wetlands;
- the cessation of pot-shots at birds of prey;
- the Irish Sea being uncontaminated by radioactive waste;
- the recognition that some of our bogs are irreplaceable treasures;
- the universal acceptance of the notion that conservation of the environment is more than a question of the future of some rare weed and may in the last analysis be the salvation of us all.

It would have been nice indeed.

the Irish Times - 16 Sep. 1985

GARDAI in Co Wicklow are investigating the callous shooting of a pair of nesting barn owls at Ballyronan, Newtownmountkennedy. The birds, which are a protected species under the 1976 Wildlife Act, were shot "for no apparent reason, except probably for target practice," said Mrs Rhoda Massey, of Ballyronan House, whose son Alan (16) found the two birds dead on the ground. Those who shot the owls, if found, face a maximum fine of £1,000 and can have their guns confiscated by the courts.

Mrs Massey said the owls had their lands for years. They ...body about them so ...have ñv in

This congress will once again focus international attention on Ireland's peatlands and hopefully, on the absence of any conservation programme for them. The real "challenge of the future" will be getting a few of them conserved.

The aftermath of the radioactive leakage from the British Nuclear Fuels Ltd. plant at Sellafield — formerly Windscale — continues to arouse concern. Materials cont...

122

In 1982 a Spanish freighter, the Ranga, ran onto the rocks on Dunmore Head, Dingle Peninsula. The crew was saved but the ship leaked oil which polluted nearby Coomenole beach. The incident was more of an inconvenience than an ecological disaster. It showed however how vulnerable our beaches are: thousands of sea-birds and much other sea life is killed each year by oil-spills and other forms of pollution.

the Ranga on Dunmore Head